Print and Production Finishes for Brochures and Catalogs

A RotoVision Book

Published and distributed by RotoVision SA
Route Suisse 9
CH-1295 Mies
Switzerland

RotoVision SA
Sales and Editorial Office
Sheridan House, 114 Western Road
Hove BN3 1DD, UK

Tel: +44 (0)1273 72 72 68
Fax: +44 (0)1273 72 72 69
www.rotovision.com

10 9 8 7 6 5 4 3 2 1

ISBN: 978-2-88893-038-9

Art Director: Tony Seddon
Design: Struktur Design Limited
Photography: Roger Fawcett-Tang

Reprographics in Singapore by ProVision Pte.
Tel: +65 6334 7720
Fax: +65 6334 7721

Printing and binding in Singapore
by Star Standard Industries (Pte) Ltd.

I would like to extend my deep thanks to all those who
have helped in creating this book, whether by kindly
submitting work, or through their help and support.

Print and Production Finishes for Brochures and Catalogs

Roger Fawcett-Tang

RotoVision

Contents

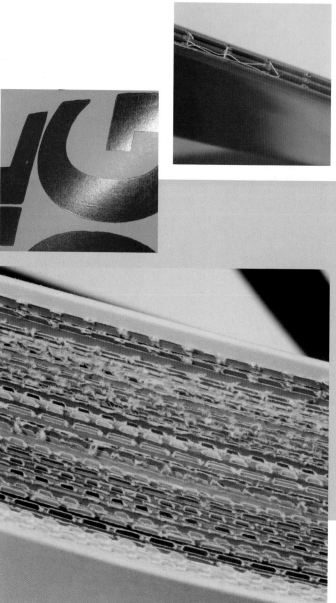

Looking through the vast quantity of showcase-style books on graphic design, the diversity of design styles and production techniques can at times seem daunting. Often, work is shown with little or no information about how the effects were achieved, or a technique that you may not be familiar with, such as "half Canadian bound–cover with a spot UV varnish," is flippantly mentioned. The aim of this book is to demystify the jargon used and the production processes utilized by many of the world's top designers. While giving names to techniques you may already have come across, the book also shows more unusual printing and production methods that you may not have encountered before.

Quite often the most rudimentary of production techniques can be used, but by giving additional thought to the materials used in, or the size of a project, the result can become something that rises above the commonplace. By developing a greater understanding of the conventional off-set litho printing methods, the designer can see how the system can be adjusted to meet his needs. Two-color printing can be used to help reduce printing costs and can often result in a far richer product as the colors are flat and solid. The pigments are more vibrant than a color achieved out of CMYK, which is made up of tinted values of the four process colors. Overprinting two colors can also produce interesting effects that are unique to the process.

The choice of materials can have a striking effect on the product. Consideration should always be given to the substrate. Changing the weight, color, or finish can achieve a great effect on the finished work. As designers focus more and more on the screen-based virtual world of

brochure design, it is easy to neglect the tactile quality of the finished work. Think about the way the pages will be planned-up on the printer's plates (imposition). Maybe some sections of a brochure or catalog don't need to be printed 4-color process; perhaps additional special fifth or sixth colors could be added to certain sections or plates that will not necessarily appear on consecutive pages in the final bound document.

What are the effects of printing onto very thin (bible) paper, or even coated stocks that have a greater degree of showthrough. This can be used to your advantage; by being aware of what can be seen, and the density and shape of objects on the pages following, the design can work to hide and reveal shapes as the pages are turned.

A creative solution is often possible, whatever the print budget. By reducing the physical size of a brochure, the designer can save on printer's plates and paper costs. This saving can then be used to cover the cost of a better

binding technique, paper quality, or additional colors. By building a good knowledge of the printing industry, the designer will gain a clearer understanding of the costs associated with different printing processes. This will enable him/her to design in the most cost-effective manner.

Hopefully, this book will inspire you to create more visually rich design for print, whether for a 1-color booklet or a 6-color corporate brochure.

Formats

Design	Cartlidge Levene
Project	Sergison Bates architects
	Brick-work: Thinking and Making
Specification	136 pages plus casebound cover
	printed 2 colors and 3 colors
	thread-sewn sections

Produced to accompany an exhibition in Zurich of the architect's work, this book works purely with photographs of scale models of the various building projects. Simply printed in black and warm gray, the scale models are given a dark, nocturnal quality. Each project is introduced by a four-page section printed on a reduced-size page, which features diagrammatic details of the building's construction. These smaller pages are also printed in black and warm gray, but with a very pale, warm gray background. The cover of this casebound book uses a black bookbinding cloth, with the title blocked in white and gray; the image is tipped-in to a debossed area on the cover.

Reduced page size

Each project is introduced with a 4-page section printed on a reduced-size page which features diagrammatic details of the building's construction. These pages hide and reveal elements on the full-size pages of the main body of the book.

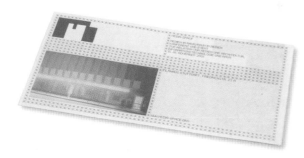

Design	Projekttriangle
Project	Media-Space leaflet
Specification	16-page folded leaflet
	printed 2 colors
	part folded, part unfolded

Produced to accompany a four-day conference in new
media in Stuttgart, Germany. A bitmap font is used for the
headlines and general text, with an X-style bitmap dingbat
used in various repeat patterns throughout the leaflet.
Printed in red and green on a very light weight of uncoated
paper (bible). This permits a great deal of showthrough,
which the designers have been fully aware of and have
used to their advantage. Large areas of the leaflet are
printed with blocks of solid color, repeated patterns
of the X dingbat, or blocks of small dots forming
coarse halftone areas.

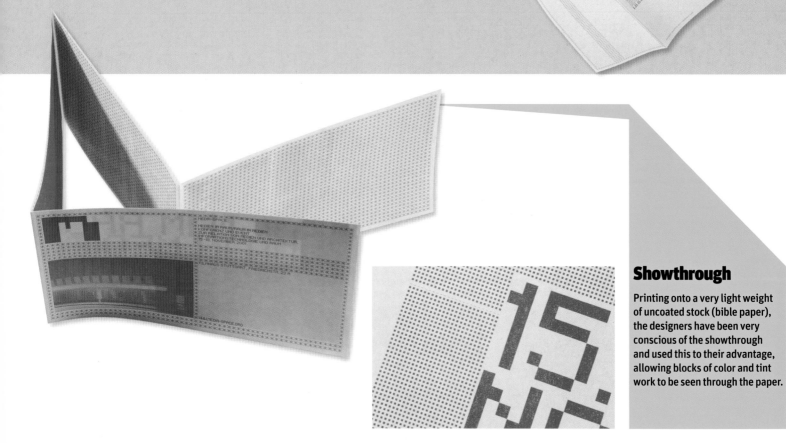

Showthrough

Printing onto a very light weight
of uncoated stock (bible paper),
the designers have been very
conscious of the showthrough
and used this to their advantage,
allowing blocks of color and tint
work to be seen through the paper.

Progressive page widths

The pages of this booklet become
progressively wider, which creates
an indexing system and also
displays a full contents list when
the booklet is still closed.

Design	sans+baum
Project	Take Control of Your Asthma
Specification	52 pages plus 6-page cover
	printed 6 colors
	saddle-stitched

This is printed in a total of six special colors, which enables
each section of this health information booklet to have its
own color. This large selection of colors is made possible
by planning the sections of the booklet in such a way that
some sections are printed in 2-color and others in 3-color;
a dark maroon is used throughout the book to give a strong
consistency, and all the portraits are printed in this maroon
too. The pages are trimmed at different widths to permit
a sequence of tabbed section dividers to work, and this
has the added benefit of showing a contents list from
the front cover.

Design	Nokia Design Brand Team
Project	Pure Ideas
Specification	92 pages plus 48 small-format pages, 4-page cover and dust jacket printed 1 color and 4-color process plus various specials and varnishes perfect-bound

Produced as an internal document for Nokia, this brochure visually catalogs the research and development of the newly formed Nokia Design Brand Team. A minimal white cover conceals the lavishly produced contents held within. The cover has the title foil blocked in a clear varnish, with the Nokia logo printed in blue at the foot of the cover; and a dust jacket wraps around the cover, which unfolds into a large poster. Inside, the brand's corporate colors of white, blue, and green are introduced by a single sheet of an uncoated green stock. This is followed by a 16-page section on a pale blue uncoated stock printed in the corporate blue, and this section contains an interview with three key members of the design team. The brochure then switches to a coated silk stock as it visually illustrates the corporate colors, typography, photographic treatments, and graphic treatments, and finally ends with a series of images from the design studio. Throughout the brochure are a series of small pages printed on a light weight of cast-coated stock (gloss on one side and matte on the reverse). The brochure makes extensive use of a spot machine varnish and a color-tinted machine varnish to highlight areas of the page, echoing the size and position of the small inset pages or used as borders for full-bleed images, and so on.

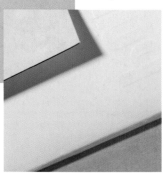

Inset pages

A series of inset pages appear throughout the brochure, always trimmed flush to the base of the book. These pages are used to provide additional information on the design principles. Even on pages without this inset page, the same area is often highlighted in a UV varnish.

White

Design	Struktur Design
Project	PSD: International Recruitment Services
Specification	42 pages plus 4-page cover
	printed 5 colors
	die-cut
	concertina-folded sections

The brief from the client was to create a brochure that could work both as a conventional "leave-behind" brochure and as a presentation document. The key message that the client was keen to communicate was the "breadth and depth" of the company's services as one of the UK's leading professional human-resource companies. The design took this key message to heart in creating a concertina-folded document that can be unfolded to more than 3.5m (11ft) in length, thereby visually showing the company's "breadth." A square window is die-cut in each page of the brochure, revealing the company's square logo, which is printed on the inside back cover; this helps to illustrate the company's "depth" and enables their logo to appear on every spread of the brochure.

Die-cut

Each page of this concertina-folded brochure features a die-cut square, in the same size and position, through which can be seen the company's logo which is printed on the inside back cover.

Design	Surface/Miwa Yanagi
Project	Miwa Yanagi monograph
Specification	44 pages plus 78 pages
	printed 4-color process and black only
	concertina-folded and perfect-bound

This monograph for the Japanese artist Miwa Yanagi incorporates two very different elements. Within the six-page, gatefold cover is a concertina-folded color section on the left, and on the right, a monochromatic textbook with small, black-and-white reproductions of the work together with a series of essays and interviews.

The concertina section is unusual in the way the images and text are positioned; both image and text wrap around the folded pages, encouraging the reader to unfold and extend the spreads. The front of the concertina section shows one series of images set on a white background, and the reverse shows another series set on black.

Double-hinged cover

Two very different books are housed within the same cover; the 3-panel cover allows for two spines. The left book extends as a long, concertina-folded section, while the right book is more conventionally bound.

Design	Browns
Project	NorthSouthEastWest: A 360° View of Climate Change
Specification	**184 pages plus casebound cover**
	printed 2 colors and 4-color process
	thread-sewn sections

Produced for the British Council and the Climate Change Group, this beautiful, photographically heavy book captures the devastating effects of climate change. The minimal typographic cover plays with the orientation of the book, with all text and images running at 90 degrees to the spine. Inside, the book starts on an uncoated stock printed in black and red, with the injection of an occasional full-color page; this is followed by a series of photographs from around the world, printed onto a coated silk stock.

Varnish and simulator

This book uses white simulator paper with the text printed in black and gold. Machine and spot UV varnishes are employed to add greater depth to the illustrations.

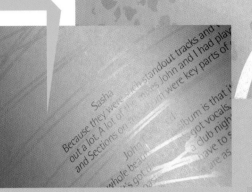

Design	The Kitchen
Project	Renaissance: The Mix Collection
Specification	36 pages plus casebound cover
	printed 4-color process plus UV and
	machine varnishes
	sewn-through sections

To accompany the tenth anniversary of the nightclub/record label Renaissance, The Kitchen avoided CD packaging methods and opted for an extremely long, thin, panoramic-format book. The format is derived from the placement of three CDs end-to-end on the inside back cover. Elaborate full-color illustrations formed from fragments of previously released CDs are given greater depth by floral elements, which are printed using a "dirty" varnish. The book is broken into different sections, each of which is divided by a sheet of thick, white simulator paper with the title printed on it in black and gold type. The book is thread-sewn "sewn through"—a binding method achieved by sewing from front to back, forming a very strong bind.

22

Design	Base Design
Project	Women'secret: Look Book Automne 03
Specification	6 folded posters plus cover folder
	printed 4-color process

This 4-leafed folder opens to reveal a series of six separate folded sheets, each shot by a different photographer. The sheets are printed on one side of a thin, cast-coated stock only; the uncoated side is left unprinted which gives a strong, tactile contrast to the sheen of the photography. The front panel of each folded poster is printed with a strong background color with the title, photographer's name, and a brief introduction printed in contrasting colors. When unfolded the posters measure 625 x 440mm (24²/₃ x 17¹/₃in). The folds work as a grid for framing the images, although each poster uses this grid system in a different manner to express the photography in a variety of ways. The card folder is printed onto a coated board, 4-color process on the outside, and black only on the inside. A sequence of images is printed full bleed on each of the panels, allowing the color and black-and-white images to work together.

Folded sheets

Held within a card folder are
a series of six folded sheets,
each featuring photographs
of the collection by a different
photographer. The creases form
the basic grid system used
to frame the images.

Design	Oliver Walker
Project	Levi's Vintage Clothing: Reel Revolution
Specification	16-panel folded sheet plus slipcase
	printed 4-color process, cover screenprinted in 1 color
	embossed

Housed inside a custom-made, grayboard slipcase, this book for Levi's Vintage Clothing has a very loose graphic style. The slipcase is screenprinted in a single color, with the title printed and embossed to add a tactile dimension to the piece. A circular, die-cut hole reveals some hand-written text on the folded brochure within. Inside are two more sheets of the same grayboard with recesses cut to hold a series of 35mm slides. Not only do these show the fashion collection off to good effect, but also, as the pack is sent out to fashion journalists, they can be used for reproduction in magazines. Also included is a 16-panel, folded brochure with cut-up images from the collection montaged with scribbled comments and doodles. One of the panels has another sheet of grayboard affixed, with a die-cut circle used to hold a CD in place.

Slipcase

The broadsheet and 35mm transparencies are housed within a toploading slipcase. The transparency sheet is formed by bonding two sheets of grayboard together. The top sheet features a series of die-cut holes of the exact shape and size required to hold the transparencies.

Design	Pentagram/J. Abbott Miller
Project	The Saint Louis Art Museum: Wonderland
Specification	176 pages plus 4-page cover, 10 folded posters, and polypropylene slipcase printed 2 colors and 4-color process holographic-foil blocked thread-sewn sections

Producing an art catalog for a series of artist's installations can involve major logistical problems. How do you show installation views that may not be constructed by the time the catalog has to go to press? This issue has been cleverly resolved by splitting the catalog into two sections. The main, bound catalog contains essays about the various artists, together with images of their previous works. The catalog is complemented by a series of 10 folded broadsheets, one for each of the participating artists, which include images from the installations and additional information. The printing lead time for these sheets is much shorter than that for the main catalog, allowing them to be produced much closer to the opening of the exhibition.

The catalog and 10 folded sheets are housed in a translucent plastic slipcase, with the title of the exhibition printed in black outline on the front. The title also appears on the front of the catalog, printed as a holographic, silver foil blocking, which matches its position on the slipcase.

WONDER

Holographic foil

The title of this catalog is foil blocked in a special silver holographic foil that reflects a wide spectrum of colors when caught in the light.

Design	Design Project
Project	Situation Leeds: Contemporary Artists and the Public Realm 05 05
Specification	36 pages, self cover plus adhesive kiss-cut sticker sheet printed 2 colors and 3 colors saddle-stitched and folded

The simple folding in half of this saddle-stitched leaflet forms a unique format for this festival guide. The title and front cover effectively start on the back of the piece and, when unfolded, extend onto the real front of the booklet. The central crease down each page acts as a division allowing information for two separate events to appear per page. Printed on an uncoated pink stock in fluorescent pink and silver, the strong typography is accompanied by a simplified graphic map of the city center, printed in fluorescent orange on the cover. A detailed map of the city is bound in at the centerfold of the booklet, with all the locations for the various events highlighted. This map is printed in fluorescent orange and pink on the back of an adhesive sheet. The other side of this is printed full bleed in the orange and features a series of small, kiss-cut circles that can be peeled off and applied to the events pages, to check off events that you have seen or intend to see.

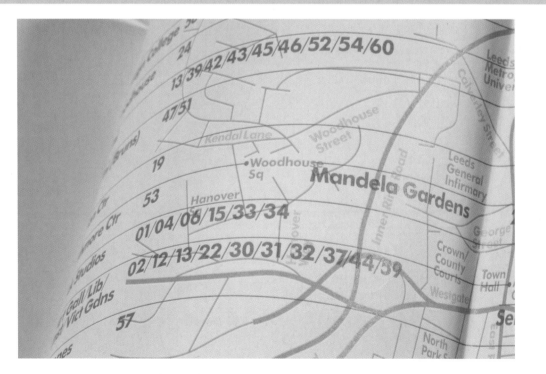

Double folded

The catalog is saddle-stitched and then folded in half, creating folded divisions on the page. This format makes a more convenient size to carry around events, and lends it a map-like quality.

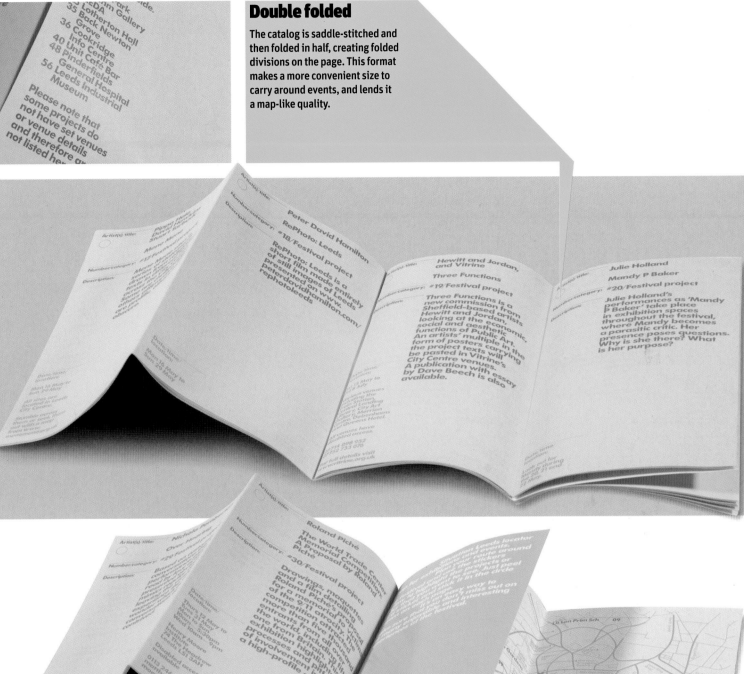

Design	Dowling Design
Project	University of Lincoln: Applicant's Guide 2006
Specification	24 pages, self-cover
	printed 4-color process
	saddle-stitched

The square format of this university guide is enhanced by a series of cropped pages on the cover, the first six pages all being cut to a narrower width, enabling the university's logo to remain visible as each successive page is turned. The rest of the guide has all the pages cropped to the full width, although visually a clear strip is left on both the left and right edges, which is used for titles and notes.

Design	Struktur Design
Project	Alamy: Two Sides to Every Story
Specification	2 x 32-page books in a 4-page cover
	printed 4-color process
	saddle-stitched

Produced to promote the two different types of images (royalty-free and licenced) of this photo library, the catalog is formed of two A6 (105 x 148mm/4¹/₈ x 5⁷/₈in) 32-page books that are bound into the same cover. From the outside, the catalog has the appearance of one tall, narrow book, but as the cover is opened, the two separate books are revealed: one stacked above the other. The imagery in each small book has a relationship to the other, with the occasional image bled off one book onto the other.

Split pages

Two small booklets are saddle-stitched, one above the other, into a single, outer cover section. This format allows the booklets to work independently, though at times images bleed from one book to the other, creating a close relationship between the two.

Design	Spin
Project	The Photographers' Gallery: Great 62
Specification	24 pages plus 4-page cover
	printed 4-color process plus special
	saddle-stitched

The Photographers' Gallery in London has produced
a quarterly catalog for many years. Over the years it has
been given a variety of designs and formats from different
design companies. The latest strips back and simplifies the
design to a very pure, minimal state. The cover is trimmed
shorter than the contents by 20mm (¾in), which allows
the top edge of the first page to appear as part of the cover.
For each issue a different lead color is chosen, sometimes
printed out of a 4-color set, sometimes a special. The first
page of the contents is always printed full bleed in the
chosen color, with the title and issue number of the
catalog printed white-out at the top.

34

Design	sans+baum, illustrations by Russell Bell
Project	Civic Trust Awards 40th Anniversary booklet
Specification	40 pages, self-cover
	printed 5 specials
	saddle-stitched

This very small booklet, produced to celebrate the
40th anniversary of the Civic Trust Awards in the United
Kingdom, is contained in shrink-wrapped plastic. Once the
plastic has been removed, it becomes apparent that the
booklet requires some interaction in order for its contents
to be read. Formed from a single sheet of paper, the booklet
has been folded and saddle-stitched, but the folded edges
have not been trimmed down. The user must finish this
process in order to read the material. The cover includes
instructions on how to "remove wrapping, cut along dotted
line, read pages from left to right." The booklet is printed in
three different specials on either side of the sheet; green,
turquoise, and black on one side and orange, purple, and
black on the other. Due to the nature of the folded sheet,
some spreads are in three colors and others in five.

Trimming

A thick, white, dotted line is printed on the three sides of the booklet that require trimming. With these edges trimmed off, the book becomes usable in a conventional manner.

Design	MadeThought
Project	Reiss: Autumn & Winter 2005
Specification	16 pages, self-cover
	printed 4-color process
	saddle-stitched

This large-format fashion catalog is printed onto an uncoated stock in full color, with the text and cover both printed on the same weight of paper. The large photographs are intercut with big diagonal strips of white, which help to separate the images and provide space for caption text.

Design	Chalet Alpin
Project	Ken 360
Specification	**80 pages plus cover**
	printed 2 colors and 4-color process
	folded sheet

The designers have used a standard folding map as a reference point for this project, produced for a new series of travelog brochures/magazines. The format enables the different panels of text and imagery to be read easily and echoes the sense of adventure associated with a folded map. It also makes the piece less precious and more user-interactive than a conventionally bound document. The scale of the sheet is used to good effect on the reverse, which is printed just in warm gray and blue, showing a huge monotone reproduction of one of the images from the front.

Materials

N° D'ARTICEL

256-A

N° DE COMMANDE

640 SB 5

N° D'UNITE

42

WEIGHT/GEWICHT/POIDS

599

91118003

PRODUCT/PRODUKT/PRODUIT

ACCENT ART

MARK/SIGNUM/MARQUAGE

3034298

Stock Desc: WRA VOYAGER GLOSS

Slot Number: 77271

Load Number: 7683

PO Number: 91118520

Making Number:

Size: 450X640

Type B

Substance: 0130

Quantity: 1000lb

Account: JMC

Footprint: A2

Mon Dec: 5.06.49:52.2005

1000787959 1861

Design	Kapitza
Project	Janet Hodgson: The Pits
Specification	124 pages plus casebound cover and dust jacket
	printed 1 color and 4-color process
	sewn sections

The artist Janet Hodgson was commissioned by Land Securities in partnership with Canterbury City Council, UK, to create a permanent artwork related to the archeological digs that took place over a four-year period in Canterbury. The book brings together fragments of the artist's process over this period. It is punctuated by different sections on different paper stocks, and switches between black-and-white and 4-color process. The most striking element of the book is a series of sections printed onto simulator paper, which show fragments of the archeologists' site maps charting the progress of each individual hole in the dig. These hand-drawn information maps were photographed and color-treated by the designers to create a series of richly colored layers. The book also makes good use of the contrast between the heavy black-and-white text

pages and the vibrant full-color coated pages, which illustrate the work of other artists involved in the project, together with images of Janet Hodgson's final work—based on the maps used by the archeologists, Janet commissioned stone masons to carve these organically shaped maps onto the final footpath.

The cover of this lovely book is casebound, with simple gray bookbinding boards, which have been screenprinted with the title of the project in white. The book is then wrapped in a simulator-paper dust jacket, again printed in richly colorful impressions of the site maps, with barely decipherable scribbled notes about the progress of the dig. The text printed on the grayboards is also semi-visible through this layer.

amme to
ning Department
guard the development

et Hodgson was invited to
role during September 2
ough a competitive inter
e demonstrated her app
actice which both excite

e brief offered to Jane
 be too prescriptive. It
me to research and de
hrough dialogue and a
and the City of Canter

What this book will d
were possible as a re
of the project team

From a relatively n
development grev
Council England
Canterbury City

Sam Wilkinson

Layers

Throughout the book, sections of
simulator paper are used. These show
fragments of the site maps charting
the progress of each hole in the dig.
These hand-drawn information maps
have been photographed and color-
treated by the designers to create
a series of richly colored layers.

Design	SEA Design
Project	Staverton
Specification	24 pages plus 4-page cover
	printed 4-color process plus UV varnish
	heat welded
	Singer-sewn section

This text-light brochure for a London-based office furniture manufacturer conveys all the information required through beautifully clean photography and high production values. Every page of the brochure is printed with a full-bleed UV gloss varnish, which evokes the quality and high production values of the furniture.

The brochure is Singer-sewn, whereby an industrial sewing machine is used to bind it; a line of matching yellow thread runs down the central crease, forming a very strong binding. The brochure's cover is made from a soft, flexible PVC, with the company's logo heat-welded onto the front. The cover is bonded to the first and last pages of the brochure, thereby hiding the thread on the spine. It becomes seamless with the text pages, because the color match of PVC yellow and litho-printed yellow are spot on.

Design	SEA Design
Project	Matthew Williamson: Five Years in Fashion
Specification	16 pages plus 4-page cover
	printed 4-color process
	embossed with holographic film treatment
	saddle-stitched

To celebrate five years in the business, fashion designer Matthew Williamson wanted to produce a retrospective catalog of his past ten collections. He selected 11 of his favorite pieces and asked a selection of high-profile women to model for him, including the likes of Jade Jagger, Gwyneth Paltrow, and Helena Christensen. With Rankin taking the shots, this simple little catalog oozes fashion status. The cover just has Williamson's name embossed across the bottom, but is striking because of the use of a special holographic film, which is laminated to the surface of the board; the film comes in a selection of color biases, and for this cover the designers chose pink.

Holographic film

The title of the catalog is simply embossed across the bottom, but becomes alive through the use of a special holographic film, which is laminated to the surface of the board. The film comes in a selection of color biases.

Design	**Eggers + Diaper**
Project	**Rachel Lichtenstein:**
	Add. 17469: A Little Dust Whispered
Specification	**96 pages plus casebound cover**
	printed 4-color process
	foil blocked
	thread-sewn sections

Artist and writer Rachel Lichtenstein's research into old and forgotten manuscripts found in the huge archives of the British Library, London, led to this publication and an accompanying exhibition in the British Library. As the first Creative Research Fellow of the Library, she was able to gain access to the vast collection of ancient manuscripts dating back to the fourth century. The resulting book shows full-bleed images of these fragmented manuscripts, alongside a running text printed in black with captions in cyan and red. The book is printed on a cream cotton stock, which is light and yet dense, and it therefore has a thickness disproportionate to its light weight. The pages are interspersed with a thin bible paper printed in red, which helps to add another layer to the book.

Design	MadeThought
Project	Established & Sons: 100% Design Tokyo invitation
Specification	8 pages plus 6-page cover
	printed 1 color
	foil blocked
	saddle-stitched

Produced as an invitation to an exhibition of the company's work in Tokyo, this simple leaflet follows on from the main product catalog in style and content, but is printed just in black onto a thin, uncoated, plain gray stock. The company's logo is foil blocked in white on the front cover to help lighten the impact of all the large, black typography. The leaflet is saddle-stitched using white-coated wires, to pick up on the white, foil-blocked logo.

Design	Eggers + Diaper
Project	Aï Kitahara: Works 1992–2005
Specification	128 pages plus 8-page cover
	printed 1 color and 4-color process
	thread-sewn sections

A tactile reaction is experienced as soon as this catalog is picked up. The front cover features a die-cut aperture, which reveals a sheet of coarse sandpaper, creating great contrast with the smooth, white, matte-laminated cover. The catalog shows the work of Aï Kitahara, a Japanese artist living in Paris, and the book is therefore printed as a trilingual text, in English, Japanese, and French. The pictogram on the cover is a motif frequently used by the artist (as is sandpaper). Inside, a full-color image section is sandwiched between mono text sections at the front and back of the book.

Die-cut and sandpaper

The front cover features a die-cut aperture that reveals a sheet of coarse sandpaper, creating great contrast with the smooth, white, matte-laminated cover.

Design	MadeThought
Project	Established & Sons: Liberty invitation
Specification	16-panel folded sheet
	printed 1 color
	foil blocked

Produced as an invitation to celebrate a retail partnership with Liberty in London, this invite is formed from a single sheet of very thin bible paper folded down to a manageable format. The sheet is printed in black with a copper foil block used to highlight the event.

Also shown is an invitation for a UK launch during Design Week. This invite is a single sheet of grayboard, screen-printed on both sides with white ink. Again, the company's logo is foil blocked in copper.

Design	Eggers + Diaper
Project	Kutlug Ataman: Küba
Specification	170 pages plus 40 sheets of onionskin paper
	printed 4-color process
	ring binder flocked and foil blocked
	loose-leaf sheets in a ring binder

Küba is the name of an anarchistic shanty town in Istanbul, where the filmmaker Kutlug Ataman interviewed 40 inhabitants, ranging from left-wing militants to right-wing religious groups, feminists, gays, and so on. The interviews were shown in an installation that featured each of the 40 talking heads appearing on 40 old television sets, arranged with old chairs and sofas in a large space, reflecting the dishevelled nature of Küba. The installation was shown in London, Pittsburgh, Stuttgart and Vienna. The accompanying catalog, which was designed as a kitsch photo album to reflect something of the nature of Küba, consists of a loose-leaf binder, finished in purple and deep red flocking, with the title foil blocked in silver. Inside, the catalog is printed in 4-color process onto an uncoated cream stock, which gives the book a soft, tactile quality.

Each of the 40 interviews appears with a transcript and photographs, and the text is set in an old typewriter font, with corrections crossed out and overtyped, which gives the book a low-tech appearance appropriate to the work. The interviews are divided from each other by a sheet of thin onion-skin glasscene paper—the same stock that is used in old photograph albums to protect the images.

Onionskin

The interviews are divided from each other by a sheet of thin onionskin glasscene paper—the stock that is used in old photograph albums to protect the images.

Design	MetaDesign London
Project	Transig
Specification	24 pages plus 4-page cover
	printed 6 specials
	Singer-sewn through

This brochure was used as a launch tool for Transig, a new rail operator in the United Kingdom. The brochure utilizes the 45° angles of the wordmark; these appear as a series of parallel lines throughout the pages, as a reference to the rail tracks. The brochure is purely printed in specials: green, red, yellow, gray, white, and black. With the exception of the gray, which is used to reproduce a series of halftone images, all the other colors are applied as flat, solid inks, without any tint work. All the pages use thick tracing paper, and are French-folded, which makes the whole brochure multilayered: as each page is turned, different elements become clearer. The insides of the French-folded pages are printed in two colors: gray and white. The gray is used for large section titles and is also used to reproduce various industrial images. The white ink is printed full bleed on the page as a method of increasing the opacity of the brochure. The outside of the French-folds is printed in red, green, yellow, and black. The sheets are Singer-sewn through which gives a very strong binding. A 4-page cover, printed in the same red, green, and yellow inks on an uncoated board, is drawn onto the folded contents.

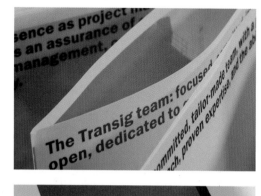

Design	sans+baum
Project	The Architecture Foundation: Who We Are
Specification	16 pages
	printed 1 color and 3 colors
	folded sheet

Through a very strong use of color, this simple typographic folded sheet has great visual impact. Printed onto a very light weight of uncoated stock, the solid blocks of heavy color play against the slabs of white areas that allow showthrough from the other side. The reverse side is printed full bleed in one color only, and again the blocks of color and white areas are partially visible.

Design	**Carsten Nicolai/Olaf Bender/Jonna Groendahl**
Project	**Carsten Nicolai: Auto Pilot**
Specification	**104 pages plus 8-page cover** **printed 1 color and 4-color process** **heat-welded, laser cut, die-cut** **thread-sewn sections**

This book by and about the artist, musician, producer, designer, and record-label founder Carsten Nicolai shows a close affinity with his audio and visual projects. Both his sound and installation-based artwork strip back elements to a total minimum, an ideology that is reflected in the clean, minimal design of the book. The book contains a CD of his audio works, which is housed within the gatefolded front cover. A die-cut circle in the front cover reveals the central spindle, and a small circle of bright yellow from the disk's surface. This fragment of vibrant color creates a strong contrast to the rest of the understated book. Toward the front of the book an abstract arrangement of dots that relates to a piece of the artist's work has been

laser cut into the page. Further on, a 16-page section of clear acetate sheet has been heat-welded and bound into the book. These sheets feature a series of blocks of solid black printed on them. The blocks are divided up as half pages, quarter pages and eighths so that, as the acetates are turned, the density of black increases and decreases.

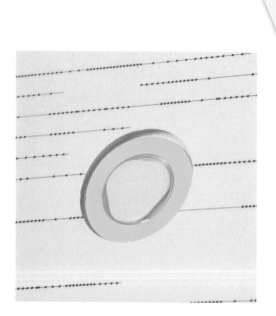

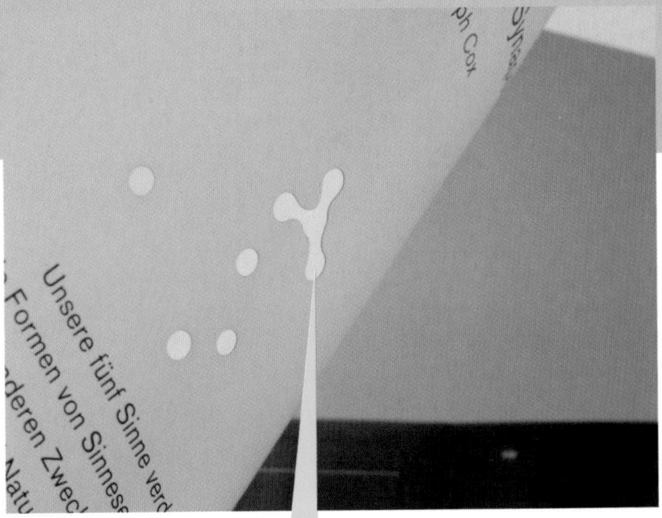

Unsere fünf Sinne verd
Formen von Sinnes
deren Zwec
Natu

Laser die-cut

A series of small, organically shaped holes are laser cut into one of the pages of this book. The edges of the cut become scorched by the laser during this process.

Design	Spin
Project	Keith Tyson: History Paintings
Specification	92 pages plus casebound cover
	printed 3 specials plus mono section
	cover flocked
	thread-sewn sections

Produced to accompany an exhibition at the Haunch of Venison gallery in London, this large, landscape book is an appropriate format to house a series of large paintings and give an added sense of scale to the works. Some of the larger paintings are produced on gatefold pages. The paintings all use a limited palette of colors: red, green, black, and white. After initial trials with 4-color reproduction, the designers decided that the best method of reproducing the images as faithfully as possible was to print them in three special colors; the result is strikingly beautiful. As a contrast to the very graphic and colorful plate section, a series of black-and-white reproductions of newspapers is printed at the back of the catalog on an uncoated stock. The cover of the book forms another contrast, to both the hard-lined, graphic, abstract paintings and the retro newspapers. Casebound with a flock finish, two versions were produced, one red and one black, according to the general color palette.

Design	Faydherbe/De Vringer
Project	Underware: Dolly
Specification	32 pages plus 8-page cover
	printed 4-color process
	cover flocked and foil blocked
	thread-sewn sections

This type-specimen book was produced in two versions: the standard version featured a cover printed in fluorescent pink with the dog motif foil blocked in silver. The limited-edition version, given out at the launch party for the font, came in a flocked, burgundy cover, again foil blocked in silver. On both versions, the inside front flap features a die-cut slit which houses a demonstration version of the font. The text pages feature a variety of different potential applications for the new font, from medical textbooks to dictionaries and old picture books.

Design	Spin
Project	D&AD Annual 2005
Specification	592 pages plus casebound cover
	printed 4-color process
	thread-sewn sections

This edition of the D&AD Annual saw the first redesign of the internal pages in a long period. Each year a different design company or advertising "guru" is invited to design the annual, however, the design is usually limited to just the cover and divider pages; the rest of the hefty tome is left untouched. This annual featured a total design application, from outer packaging to all text pages. The general concept was to highlight the gritty reality of the awards and annuals process, showing the journey photographically from submission of work, through judging process, to final awards ceremony. Inside the simple brown cardboard packaging the book is wrapped in a large poster which features a call for enteries for the next year's awards. The cover features a quarter-bound cloth cover, where the bookbinding cloth is applied to the spine and wraps around onto the front and back covers.

Design	Design Project
Project	ArjoWiggins: Unusual Printing Surfaces: Experimenting with Paper, Board and Plastic Substrates
Specification	64 pages plus slipcase printed various specials, metallics, fluorescents, and varnishes perforated 3-hole sewn

This brochure was produced to show off ArjoWiggins' new range of specialist substrates, papers, plastics, and boards featuring translucents, particles, and metallics. These very unusual surfaces are printed in a wide variety of different inks, including metallics, fluorescents, and varnishes, using a series of graphic patterns and line work. A series of fine perforations die-cut into the pages add another dimension to their surface and allow the user to tear out sample swatches from the book as reference. The book is housed in a slipcase printed in a holographic, foil blocked silver, and featuring a full-length flap that contains further information about the various stocks. The slipcase is not as wide as the book it contains, which allows the book's spine to stand proud of the case.

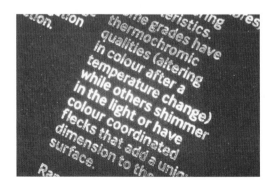

Standard printing

Design	Cartlidge Levene
Project	The Business of Design Design Industry Research 2005
Specification	112 pages plus 4-page cover printed 3 spot colors tipped-in bookmark ribbon sewn sections

Printed in red, magenta, and a dark gray, this elegant research handbook converts what could be very dry information into a rich, colorful document. The cover features a string of statistics running vertically up the page, wrapping from the back to the front cover, while the text is printed in a combination of magenta and white out of red bars. Inside, the text pages are printed on two different qualities of environmentally friendly recycled paper. The first section, which contains the bulk of the information, is printed on a cleaner, whiter stock. The back section is printed on a thinner, off-white stock, with regional maps printed in solid magenta and primary statistics printed in gray. A red ribbon is bound into the book between these two sections.

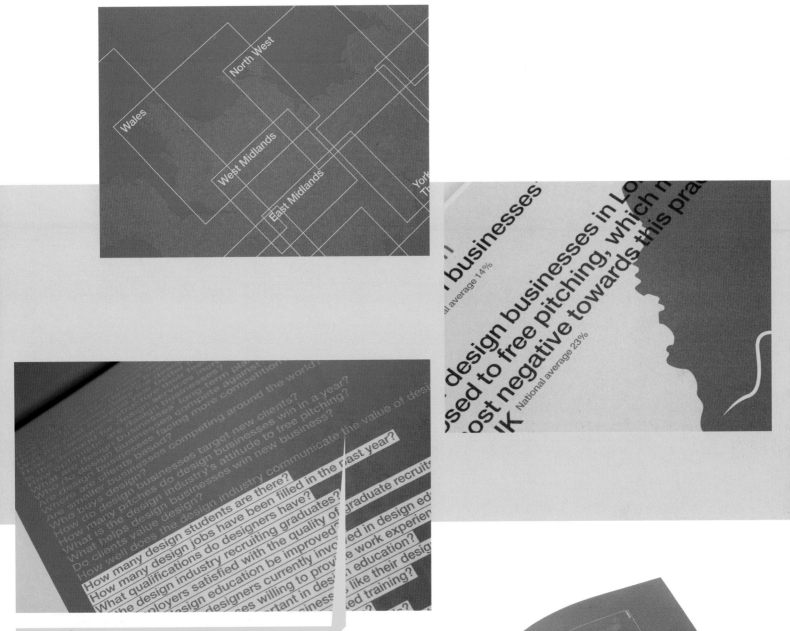

Two colors

Printed in just red and magenta, the typography becomes difficult to read as the two colors compete with each other. However, with the introduction of white strips printed behind the type, the words become far more legible.

Design	Kapitza
Project	William Morris
Specification	76 pages plus 8-page cover
	printed 1 color and 4-color process
	perfect-bound

Produced to accompany an exhibition of textile designs by the Arts and Crafts pioneer William Morris, the designers created this very fresh contemporary catalog mainly through the use of a striking palette of colors not normally associated with Morris's work. The bulk of the text pages are printed in just one color; the first section is printed in rubine red, followed by a rich earthy brown, followed by an 18-page section of full-color reproductions of Morris's textiles and related ephemera; the catalog then finishes where it started with another burst of the rubine red. It is printed on a natural off-white uncoated stock that lends itself to the archive images and adds color to the mono pages.

The text section is illustrated with digitized fragments of Morris's floral designs, which help to give a playful pace and color to the page. The cover has full-length flaps on both front and back, printed in full-bleed fluorescent pink—again a color not normally associated with the Arts and Crafts movement.

Specials and process

By combining 1-color sections printed in special colors with standard 4-color process sections, a striking contrast is made between the two printing methods. The aging textile prints are given a refreshing contemporary quality by setting them against the colorful, graphic, floral interpretations.

Design	Mode
Project	Dalton Maag: Practice Journal 2002
Specification	44 pages plus 4-page cover and dust jacket
	printed 1 color
	embossed
	saddle-stitched

A selection of custom font design case studies are showcased in this simple brochure, designed to raise the profile of this specialist font-design company. The cover, dust jacket, and initial 12-page section are all printed in dark blue on a duck-egg blue colored uncoated stock—the company's corporate color scheme. The rest of the brochure is printed in black on an off-white coated silk stock, and although the whole brochure is printed in single colors, because of the change of stock and ink color, the result is far from bland. The 12-page, pale blue section wraps around the outside of the coated stock and is simply saddle-stitched. The addition of a dust jacket in the same color, with the company logo embossed on it, ensures that the final product is beautifully finished.

Embossing

The front cover features an abstracted version of the company's logo which runs around the spine. The company's brand is also embossed into the bottom right corner.

Design	Projekttriangle
Project	Media Arts and Technology Graduate Program
Specification	8 pages plus 4-page cover
	printed 4-color process
	saddle-stitched

Printed on a crisp, white uncoated stock, this graduate program for the University of California in Santa Barbara is simply printed in 4-color process. However, the designers have made a virtue of overprinting process yellow and process cyan to form a pure green, which is used for the text and headlines. The cover features a graphic illustration formed by bitmap fragments, which are printed in yellow, with the same illustration duplicated and shifted by 1mm (1/32in) and printed in cyan, giving the image a sense of additional depth.

Design	Cartlidge Levene
Project	Bruce Nauman: Raw Materials
Specification	**144 pages plus dust jacket**
	printed 2 colors and 4-color process
	thread-sewn sections, casebound

Produced to accompany a large-scale sound installation in the Turbine Hall at Tate Modern, London, this book is broken into three clear sections. The first section contains a series of essays, with the text printed onto a warm gray uncoated stock in black and gray. The next section contains all the repeated words and phrases used in the installation, which are printed in black onto a cool gray uncoated stock. The final section is printed in full color on a gloss coated stock, and shows a selection of Nauman's other works and images, plus sketches of the preparation for the Turbine Hall installation. The book was produced as both paperback and casebound editions; the casebound version (shown here) uses a quality gray cloth with the title screenprinted on in black and gray.

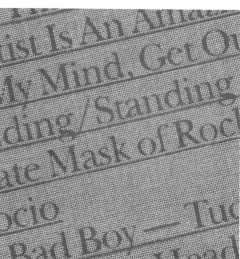

Contrasting stocks

The repeated words and phrases
used in the installation are printed
in black onto a cool gray, uncoated
stock. This is followed by a section
printed in full color on a gloss-
coated stock, showing a selection
of Bruce Nauman's other works
and images.

Design	Russell Holmes
Project	Richard Learoyd
Specification	150 pages plus 4-page cover with flaps
	printed 4-color process, machine varnish and
	gloss UV varnish
	thread-sewn sections

The understated beauty of the everyday is lovingly captured in this catalog of photographer Richard Learoyd's work. Printed 4-color process throughout, the book maintains its pace with a refreshing variety of crops and scale, from full-bleed to thumbnail images. The book also contains a number of foldout pages, which again adjust the pace and scale. Gloss machine varnishes are applied to the majority of the images, with an occasional splash of high-gloss UV varnish to add to the tactile nature of the book. The cover, printed on an uncoated board, forms a contrast to the silk pages held within.

Design	Image Now
Project	Josef Müller-Brockmann: Forty-eight Posters
Specification	112 pages plus casebound cover
	printed 4-color process plus 1 special
	embossed
	thread-sewn sections

Produced to accompany an exhibition of the same name in Ireland, this elegant catalog captures the spirit of the guru of graphic design, Josef Müller-Brockmann, while maintaining a fresh contemporary edge. The prelims, introduction, and endmatter are all printed on a very light semi-translucent coated stock. The designers have been fully aware of the nature of the paper and have positioned the type with great consideration. The main body of the catalog switches to a more substantial weight of the same paper, which makes the reader even more aware of the delicate weight of the prelim section. Each poster is printed in the same position on the recto page, with the verso printed full bleed in warm gray, with a series of comments by contemporary designers running in a column at 90 degrees to the page; some pages also contain working drawings and deconstructed elements of the final poster design. The warm gray pages help to focus the reader's attention on the recto pages, so that the commentary and surround design do not distract from the purity of the poster designs.

The casebound cover is printed in the same warm gray color, with one of Müller-Brockmann's most famous poster designs (Beethoven, 1955) embossed into the surface.

Embossing

The understated, casebound cover is printed in the same warm gray as used throughout the catalog, with one of Müller-Brockmann's most famous poster designs (Beethoven, 1955) embossed into the surface.

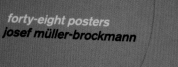

Design	Rose Design
Project	Open Systems, Rethinking Art c. 1970
Specification	192 pages plus 4-page cover
	printed 4-color process with 2- and 1-color sections
	sewn sections

This extensive catalog, produced for a major show at Tate Modern, London, is broken into three defined sections. The catalog opens with a series of essays printed onto a coated silk stock in a single dark gray, which is used for both text and image reproduction. The shift from black may be subtle in the body text, but with the halftone reproductions, the gray gives the images a faded quality. This section is followed by the main plate section, printed in four colors onto the same coated silk stock. The back of the book shifts onto an uncoated stock and features a selection of archival extracts. At first glance it would appear that this section is printed onto a gray-colored stock, because every page has a solid midtone gray color; however, the gray is printed full bleed over every page

of the archive section, and the text is printed in a dark gray color, which ties in with the essay section at the front of the catalog. Occasionally, where a piece of text is reversed out of the gray background, the white paper is revealed. The endmatter, which uses the same uncoated stock, is left white, with the text printed in the two shades of gray.

Design	Dowling Design
Project	Lamerton
Specification	12 pages plus 4-page cover **printed 1 color only** **saddle-stitched**

This is a very simple, small-format booklet to promote the work of this independent furniture-design company. Printed in silver onto a black stock, it uses keyline plans of a variety of tables to illustrate the company's range.

Design	Dowling Design
Project	Lamerton
Specification	16 pages **printed 4-color process** **die-cut and folded**

Continuing the simplicity of the black and silver booklet, this second leaflet reveals the company's furniture design through strong photography. The booklet is formed from a single sheet of A3 paper (297 x 420mm/11¾ x 16½in), which is cut and folded down to an A6 booklet (105 x 148mm/4⅛ x 5⅞in), enabling the piece to work both as a poster and as a book.

Poster/booklet

The booklet is formed from a single sheet of A3 paper (297 x 420mm /11³/₄ x 16¹/₂in), which is partially cut along the centerfold, and folded down to an A6 (105 x 148mm/4¹/₈ x 5⁷/₈in) booklet, enabling the piece to work both as a poster and as a book.

Design	**Lab Projects**
Project	**Ernesto Neto**
Specification	**48 pages plus 4-page cover**
	printed 4-color process plus 1 color
	perfect-bound

Produced to accompany a touring exhibition of the Brazilian artist/sculptor Ernesto Neto, this catalog uses typography on the cover and for the headlines inside that reflects the morphic, organic forms of the artist's work. An unusual palette of colors (including yellow, dark eggplant, and pale blue) is used throughout the catalog, and this eclectic scheme can be found to some extent in installation views of the artist's work. Printed in 4-color process, with the fluorescent yellow printed as a special, it would not be possible to obtain this vibrancy using standard-process inks. The pagination of the catalog also has a somewhat quirky feel: the conventional half-title and title pages have been replaced by images of the work, with no captions or credits, and these first three pages are then followed by more conventional prelims and a preface. Two essays follow, interspersed by more images of Neto's work. The essays are set in Bodoni and the round face is an extra-bold sans.

Design	**Duffy/Rick Sellars**
Project	**2004 Global Accounts and**
	Sector Analysis of Housing Associations
Specification	**28 pages plus 4-page cover**
	printed 2 colors
	saddle-stitched

A joint project between the Housing Corporation and the National Housing Federation in the UK, this report utilizes the main corporate color from each of the companies: purple and orange. The cover and section dividers are printed in a solid, full-bleed purple, which is overprinted with a block of the orange—the combined color is a rich, rusty brown. Some elements of the typography are reversed out of both colors, while other elements are simply reversed out of the purple, resulting in the text turning either white or orange.

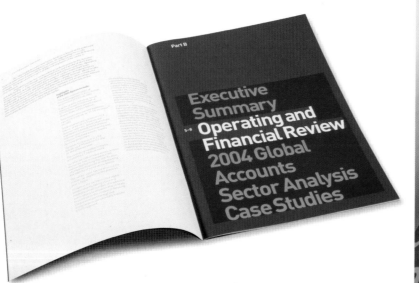

Design	Emmi Salonen
Project	35 Fragments: Contemporary Media Practice 2005
Specification	36 pages plus 8-page cover
	printed 1 color and 4-color process
	saddle-stitched

This degree-show catalog for students on the
Contemporary Media Practice course at the University
of Westminster in London avoids showing the work of
any one artist on the cover and instead opts for a clean
typographic treatment. However, on the inside of the
8-page cover a selection of full-color images is reproduced,
the only credit for these being a simple page reference
number. The text pages of the catalog are printed in black
only onto a pale blue uncoated stock.

8-page cover

All the 4-color images are
reproduced on the 8-page cover,
with the text pages simply printed
black onto a pale blue stock.

Design	**Cartlidge Levene**
Project	**Carlisle Holdings Ltd, Annual Report 2004**
Specification	**16 pages plus 4-page cover**
	printed 5 colors and 3 colors
	saddle-stitched

Printed entirely in special (not process) colors with no halftone tints, this financial report has a clean, understated quality. The only images in the brochure are reproduced as large, abstracted line art printed in a cool, light blue/gray color, helping to soften the uncompromising modern typography.

Carlisle Staffing Services operates in the UK and Ireland and provides temporary and permanent staff recruitment services as well as managed human resources solutions across a range of marketplaces. The principal strengths of the division are recognized and respected brand names, highly qualified management and staff and the ability to serve clients in many sectors.

n 1,400 hig
nned guarding se
-terrorist securit

—Sector specialist cleaning
—Manned guarding and sec
—24 hour monitoring, contr
—Retail merchandising
—Events management

Coarse halftones

To soften the purely typographic detailing, abstracted, coarse half-tone images are used. Using a diagonal line screen, the images become very abstract, readable only from a distance.

Design	Cartlidge Levene
Project	Carlisle Holdings Ltd, Annual Report 2005
Specification	12 pages plus 4-page cover
	printed 3 colors and 2 colors
	saddle-stitched

Following on from the 2004 report, the typographic treatment of the 2005 report remains largely the same, although internally there are no images, enabling the clean 2-color typography to work on its own. The cover once again relies on an abstracted halftone image, this time formed from dots as opposed to diagonal lines. The striking cover design is achieved with greater economy than that for the previous year's report, being printed with just three special colors, as opposed to the previous year's five.

Design	MadeThought
Project	Tony Cragg at Goodwood
Specification	152 pages plus casebound cover
	printed 1 color, 2 colors, 4-color process,
	and 5 colors
	thread-sewn sections

Produced to accompany an exhibition of work by the British sculptor Tony Cragg, this beautiful book follows the process of the construction and installation of his sculptures as they are placed in the rural landscape. The first 48 pages are printed on a light weight of uncoated pale blue stock, and reproduce a photographic record of the sculptures' installation. The mono images are printed in a single color that changes from section to section, starting in a rich brown, then purple, and finishing in black. Next, the book dramatically switches to a heavy, silk-coated stock, exquisitely printed in 4-color process and showing the sculptures in position. It then reverts to an uncoated white stock in a heavier weight to match that of the silk section. This section contains an essay, quotes, and a biography; the text sections are printed in black onto a pale yellow background, complemented by a series of color photographs of the artist in his studio and by images of the sculptures being constructed. The cover uses the same pale yellow background, with a landscape image of the park printed in full color, although the image has a misty quality that turns it almost mono-chromatic. The cover boards are trimmed flush to the text pages on the top and bottom edges, which gives the book a special quality.

Design	Browns
Project	Photonica: RGB
Specification	**192 pages plus casebound cover**
	printed 1 color, 2 colors, and 4-color process
	thread-sewn sections

The whole notion of RGB in CMYK throws up an interesting relationship between screen-based images and printed reality. Produced as a vehicle to steer designers toward looking at the photo library's Web site, this book shows a selection of lusciously printed images grouped into the three color categories of red, green, and blue. The color photographic sections, which are printed onto a coated silk stock, are sandwiched between a lighter weight of an uncoated stock, which is printed in a single color of red, green, or blue. These uncoated sections include text related to the particular color, plus a series of different styles of graph paper for the end user to sketch on.

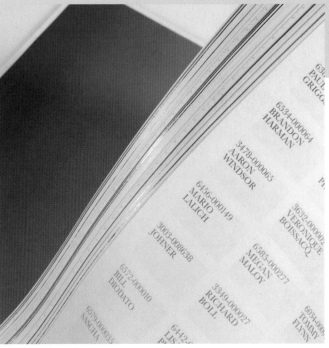

Graduated tints

Each of the three sections—red, green, and blue—are treated in the same manner, as well as showing a selection of color-coordinated photographs, the sections show sequences of tint color boxes and graduated tints, going from black to the section color.

Design	Browns
Project	Fake London Genius: Board Meeting
Specification	144 pages plus casebound covers
	printed 1 color, 4-color process, and spot machine varnish
	foil blocked
	thread-sewn sections

This book visually catalogs the development of 19 artist-designed bodyboards (small, lightweight surfboards). Nineteen artists were each given a bodyboard, which they were asked to customize. The boards were then exhibited prior to being auctioned off in aid of Greenpeace. The cover of this casebound book features a white foil block in the graphic shape of the bodyboard on a white cloth. Inside, the bulk of the book is printed on a thin, coated gloss stock in 4-color process with a machine varnish. Toward the back of the book a section of biographies and credits is printed on a light green, uncoated stock in black.

Foil blocking

The front cover features a white, foil-blocked silhouette of a body-board appearing as a ghost-like image, white on white. The embossed white foil creates a smooth area in contrast to the rest of the cover's cloth finish.

Design	**Projekttriangle**
Project	**Office launch**
Specification	**12 panels** **printed 1 color** **folded sheet**

This folded sheet maximizes the effect of using colored
stock, printed in black only, and using a quality, coated silk
stock gives the work a different feel. The three different
color variations work well together as a series.

Design	Surface
Project	Helaba
Specification	428 pages plus 4-page cover
	printed 2 colors, 4-color process, and 5 colors
	thread-sewn sections

To commemorate 50 years of collecting art, the German bank Landesbank Hessen-Thüringen produced this hefty catalog showing a selection of its vast contemporary art collection of more than 700 works by 122 artists. It diplomatically shows one work by each artist, in alphabetical order, starting with the first work on the cover. The catalog's title appears only on the spine, and the back cover carries only credits for the work shown on the front. Inside, the alphabetical sequence continues, and it is not until page 248 that the book's title appears, at which point the stock changes from a silk coated stock to an uncoated sheet; these text pages are printed with a cool gray background color printed full bleed. After these essays, the catalog shifts back to the white, coated stock and presents a series of foldout pages, which contain panoramic images of room installations. The stock then returns once again to the uncoated version with a cool gray background, and this final section includes biographies of all the featured artists, together with a series of small reproductions of all their work held in the collection.

Edge color

The designers have carefully recreated the color printed along the spine on the trimmed edges of the catalog to visually continue the color along all four edges.

Design	Spin
Project	Deutsche Börse Photography Prize 2005
Specification	112 pages plus 4-page cover and dust jacket
	4-color process
	foil blocked
	thread-sewn sections

The four photographers shortlisted for this annual prize, held at The Photographers' Gallery in London, are each given their own dust jacket for the catalog. One image by each of the photographers has been selected and used as a cover. There is no text on the front cover; the title of the event appears on the back cover on a clean white background. The same typographic treatment is used on the neutral gray card cover, foil blocked in black and gray. Inside, the catalog is printed in 4-color process, with the book split into equal parts for each of the photographers. Regardless of which version of the cover is used, the content of the catalog remains the same.

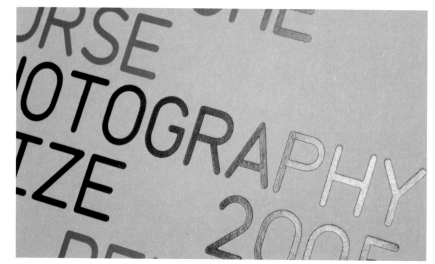

Design	Spin
Project	my-earth.org.uk
	UK Pavilion Expo 2005 Aichi, Japan
Specification	64 pages plus 8-page cover
	4-color process plus 2 specials
	thread-sewn sections

Produced to accompany the UK Pavilion at the Japanese Expo in Aichi, this brochure is printed 4-color process plus a green and a turquoise special throughout, on an uncoated stock. The two specials reflect the greenness of the United Kingdom. The 8-page cover is printed in green on the outside and turquoise on the inside. A series of coarse-line, halftone reproductions of leaves are screen-printed onto the cover in a different shade of green.

Specialist printing

Design	The Kitchen
Project	The End Biography
Specification	48 pages plus 4-page cover
	printed 2 colors and 4-color process
	foil blocked
	saddle-stitched

Produced to celebrate the tenth anniversary of the London-based nightclub "The End," this hybrid booklet created by The Kitchen is somewhere between a fanzine and a limited-edition brochure. Its slightly oversized A5 (148 x 210mm/5⅞ x 8¼in) format fits comfortably in the hand, in keeping with the scale of a fanzine-style pamphlet. The cover uses an unassuming gray board, but is transformed by the application of a large, metallic blue, foil-blocked, hand-drawn illustration, which prints full bleed and wraps around both front and back covers. The very loose illustrative style is at odds with the conventional associations of foil blocking, which has a formal heritage.

Inside, the brochure's main text section is printed in two special Pantone colors: gold and royal blue on a quality gray-colored uncoated stock. A central, 8-page section is printed onto a coated stock with full-color images. The design of the text pages contrasts classical typography with fanzine-style illustrations, again referencing the contradictive graphic language.

Foil blocking

The cover uses an unassuming gray board, but is transformed by the application of a large, metallic blue, foil-blocked, hand-drawn illustration, which prints full bleed and wraps around both front and back covers.

Design	SEA Design
Project	Identity: Private Sky
	Photography John Ross
Specification	56 pages plus 4-page cover
	printed 4-color process
	foil blocked
	French-folded pages

Commissioned by the printers Identity, based in Kent, UK, SEA Design were asked to produce a promotional booklet with a pretty open brief. Their solution was to ask photographer John Ross to take a series of images of open skies over a three-month period from January to April, to record the vast array of natural gradations and colors. These beautifully subtle, abstract color fields were then grouped month by month and sorted by color and tone. The uncoated, French-folded pages are introduced by four pages of bible paper, with the title page foil blocked in copper.

Design	SEA Design
Project	GF Smith: White Book
Specification	72 pages plus casebound cover
	printed 4-color process
	foil blocked, edge foiled
	burstbound

Produced for the paper merchants GF Smith, this beautiful book is purely a platform to enable the various different paper stocks to shine. A series of exquisite photographs of colored ink in water, taken by photographer John Ross, are reproduced in full color on each page, and because each page is a different stock, the book becomes a rich tactile experience. The final section is printed in one color only on a pale yellow stock and forms a visual record of the process of making the book. Both the cover and the endpaper at the front of the book are printed with silver foil blocking, which is picked up on the gilded edges of the book block.

Gilded edge

The trimmed edges of this book have a silver gilding applied, which relates to the silver foil blocking on the cover. This effect gives the brochure a very luxurious quality.

Design	Mode
Project	Dalton Maag: Synopsis
Specification	24 pages plus 4-page cover
	printed 2 colors
	embossed
	saddle-stitched and tipped-in

Produced to launch the new sub-brand from Dalton Maag font-design company, this book's cover and first 8-page section are printed on a high-gloss coated stock and show fragments of the new brand. The second part of the book is printed on a light gray uncoated stock, again using the same two corporate colors: pink and purple. This 16-page section contains more detailed information about the company's services. The two sections are independently saddle-stitched, then glued together with a thin strip of adhesive running close to the spine of the last page of the gloss section; the same treatment is used on the last page of the uncoated section to bind it into the cover.

The cover itself, which features fragments of the new sub-brand, uses a very fine embossed line to highlight the white keyline of the logo. This brochure was mailed out in a special foil envelope, again with fragments of the logo printed in the two vibrant colors.

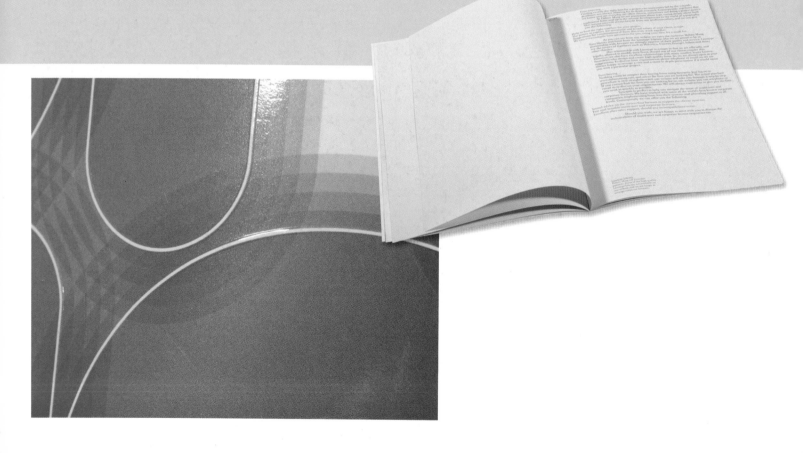

Foil packaging

The brochure is mailed out in this special silver foil bag, which is screenprinted in the two corporate colors of pink and purple. Several different variations of the bag were produced, all featuring different fragments of the logo.

Design	SEA Design
Project	Size Matters: Exploring Scale in the Arts Council Collection
Specification	72 pages plus 4-page cover
	printed 1 color, 4-color process, and spot gloss UV varnish
	matte laminated
	sewn sections

This catalog of contemporary art is fairly conventional in most respects, with essays at the front, followed by a plate section. However, the designers have chosen to print the essays section on a light blue uncoated stock, and have moved away from black and used a dark gray ink instead. This helps to give a nice contrast to the plate section, which is printed onto a quality coated silk stock.

The cover has an interesting tactile quality: the front has a matte lamination, while the back cover has been over-printed with a full-bleed gloss UV varnish. The effect, although subtle, makes the reader question the contrasting finishes. The inside front and back covers have the catalog title printed in the gloss UV varnish as a repeated pattern.

UV varnish

The inside covers have the catalog title printed in gloss UV varnish as a repeated pattern.

Design	Mode
Project	Dalton Maag: Practice Journal 2004
Specification	52 pages plus 4-page cover and wrap printed 4-color plus metallic silver perfect-bound

As a follow-up to their 2002 edition, Mode have upheld the same format and colored stock, although the production values have increased, allowing for full color throughout, plus a special metallic ink. The perfect-bound method enables a 6-page section of the uncoated pale blue stock to be slipped in toward the back of the book, as a divider between two of the case studies. The brochure is wrapped up inside a 6-page sheet of the pale blue stock, with the title printed in blue.

Design	SEA Design
Project	Colorplan
Specification	**132 pages including cover**
	printed 4-color process with specials and UV varnish
	foil blocked, die-cut
	perfect-bound with bookbinders' cloth

This small, solid block of a paper-sample book shows the full range of colors, weights, and embossed finishes available in the range. The designers show examples of a wide variety of printing techniques and effects that can be used on the stock, including 1-, 2-, 3-, and 4-color process lithography, special colors including metallics and fluorescents, foil blocking, UV varnishes, die-cutting, and embossing. The fore-edge of the book is screenprinted in silver, with the paper's names reversed out, revealing the vast spectrum of colors available in the range.

Edge printing

The book's title is screenprinted along the fore-edge of the book. The typography is reversed out of the silver ink, allowing the letterforms to adopt the multicolored block of pages. On some copies of the book the title was printed in the same manner along the spine.

Folding and creasing
Colorplan should be creased
or scored before being folded.
Always crease or score in line
with the sheet's grain, with the
ridge or bulge of the score
inside the fold.

Design	SEA Design
Project	Colorplan
	Continued from previous page.

Design	Rose Design
Project	**Whitbread: Little Black Book**
Specification	**40 pages plus 8-page cover**
	printed 4-color process plus spot UV varnish
	embossed
	sewn sections

This small information-booklet-cum-address book
for managers working within the Whitbread group of
companies in the UK is produced at a convenient small
size. The 8-page cover, printed on an uncoated board,
features the W logo embossed on the front cover, with
a spot UV varnish employed to emphasize the logo.
Fragments of handwritten diary notes are visible,
having been reversed out of the varnish.

Design	Rose Design
Project	Whitbread: WINcard Manager's Guide
Specification	48 pages plus 4-page cover
	printed 4-color process
	die-cut
	sewn sections

An internal brochure for the Whitbread group of companies, this simple booklet is enlivened by the use of a die-cut in the cover. The logo for this campaign—an uppercase W—is die-cut out of the simple white cover to reveal a series of green and orange lights on a black background. The inside front and back covers feature this photographic image printed full bleed.

Design	**A2-GRAPHICS/SW/HK**
Project	**Bad Behaviour from the Arts Council Collection**
Specification	**88 pages plus 8-page cover**
	printed 4-color process plus silver
	embossed, foil blocked, and stickered
	thread-sewn sections

The matte black cover of this catalog showcasing a collection of "potentially offensive" artworks from the collection of the UK's Arts Council has a very tactile quality, produced by a series of embossed dots on outer front and back covers. A smooth area is left for the application of a white sticker, which seals the book closed and contains all the relevant title information on both front and back. The book's title is foil blocked in silver on the spine, and the Arts Council Collection imprint is also foil blocked on the back cover. With the seal broken, the book continues the use of black on the text pages, with the essays simply printed in silver onto the black stock. This is followed by the plate section, which is printed on a coated silk stock, again using a silver ink for all caption text. At the end of the plate section is a 6-page roll-fold section, again showing more artworks, but by contrast the background is printed in solid silver with the caption details printed white out. The catalog is finished off by another section of the black stock with the silver text.

Silver on black

The text section of this art catalog is printed silver litho onto a black, uncoated stock. The strong opacity of the metallic litho ink means that it prints surprisingly well on such a dark background.

Design	Roundel Design
Project	Ikono: In Line Off Line
Specification	150 pages plus casebound cover
	printed 4-color process plus various specials and varnishes
	foil blocked, embossed, and with 4 bookmark ribbons
	thread-sewn sections

The designers were allowed to play with all the possibilities available in print when creating this book, produced to demonstrate the versatility of this range of coated paper from Zanders. The title of the book is used as a starting point for a linear device that runs horizontally across every page, either graphically or through photography. The book is divided into four sections, which relate to the four finishes in the paper range; silk, silk ivory, gloss, and matte. Each section is assigned a process color—cyan, magenta, yellow, and black—and four bookmark ribbons are bound into the book in matching colors to flag up the section breaks.

Design	Eggers + Diaper
Project	Kienholz
Specification	88 pages plus 8-page cover printed 2 colors and 4-color process plus spot UV varnish thread-sewn sections

This art catalog was produced to accompany an exhibition of husband-and-wife artists the Kienholzs, held at Baltic Centre for Contemporary Art, Gateshead, UK, and at the Museum of Contemporary Art, Sydney, Australia. The book follows a fairly conventional structure of essays, plates, and biographies, but there is a subtle shift from uncoated white stock for the text sections to a silk-coated stock for the plates, with a barely noticeable shift in the shade of white. The text sections are printed in black and a pale blue special, which is used for the headers and to form duotones for the images. The artists' work often features paint and varnish dribbles; this has been picked up by the designers and used on the front cover and inside front flap, where a large dribble of UV varnish is printed, giving the catalog a distressed appearance that echoes the artists' work.

UV varnish

A large dribble of UV varnish is printed on the front cover, giving the catalog a distressed appearance in keeping with the artists' work.

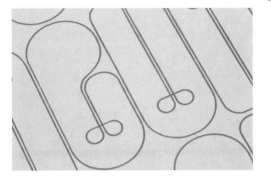

Design	Hector Pottie
Project	One two thirty
Specification	12 pages
	silkscreen printed in 1 color
	folded, unbound

This was produced to illustrate a new font design, and the designer decided simply to use the font to write the numbers from 1 to 30, to show the quirky characteristics of the font. The catalog is simply screenprinted in white onto a black board, folded, but left unbound.

Design	Hector Pottie
Project	Eins zwei fünfundzwanzig
Specification	8 pages
	silkscreen printed in 1 color
	folded, unbound

This is based on the same principle as the other font catalog, but this time the font is shown as an outline version. Again it is screenprinted, although on this occasion on pink card with magenta ink, the colors reflect the more feminine, flowery nature of the font. The text counts from 1 to 25 in German.

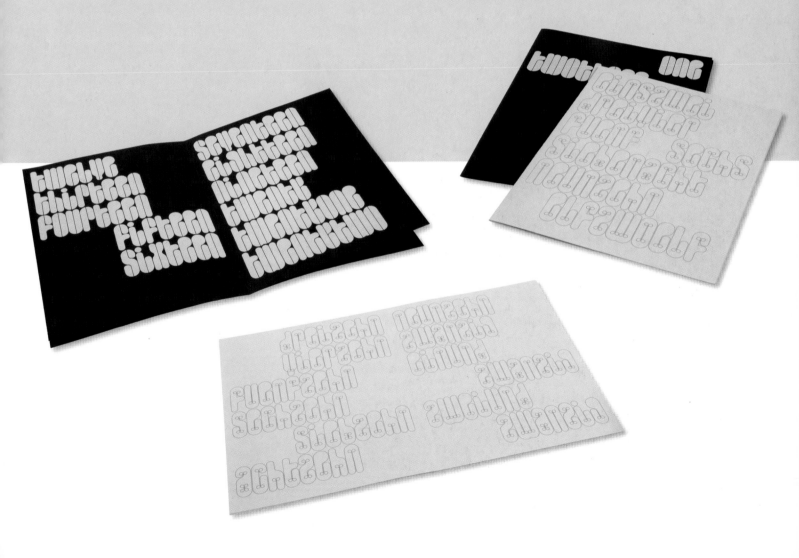

Design	Hector Pottie
Project	Home Work Social Visit Listen 1999-2003
Specification	60 pages, self cover
	screenprinted in 3 colors
	Singer-sewn through

This book was produced to accompany an exhibition in Berlin that featured a series of screenprinted maps focusing on the areas in which the designer grew up. The maps were produced as solid colors to draw attention to the beautiful coastlines and lakes.

The book uses the same screenprinted maps, but overprinted to create rich, abstract patterns. These are complemented by another mapping process, by which the designer charted his location and interests over a five-year period. A variety of cover designs appear on different copies.

Overprinting

The three screenprinted plates are overprinted on different pages, creating even more complex abstract fragments of the coastlines and typography.

Design	BB/Saunders
Project	Rankin: Fashion Stories
Specification	116 pages plus casebound cover with dust jacket
	printed 4-color process plus UV varnish
	thread-sewn sections

This large-format book of fashion photography by Rankin feels deceptively heavy for its slim extent: each page of the book is printed on heavy, coated stock, with a full-bleed, UV varnish. All this varnish adds significantly to the book's weight and also adds a striking visual and tactile effect; the pages become mirrorlike and plasticized. The dust jacket is printed in solid black with the book's title embossed around the front and back. The cover is also treated to a UV varnish printed full bleed, with the book's title discreetly screenprinted in a dark gray on the upper right side of the front cover. A list of contents is printed in the same manner on the inside flap, which also holds a perforated strip that can be used as a bookmark. On the reverse of the dust jacket is a full list of credits for each of the fashion stories, printed in a gloss UV varnish. Each of the eight fashion stories is introduced with a black, double-page spread, with the title reversed out of the UV varnish in a decorative font. Page numbers are reversed out of the UV varnish on every right-hand page.

Design	Ph.D
Project	Dickson's: The Science of Sensation
Specification	16 pages plus inserts and cover
	printed 4-color process
	letterpress printed, thermographed, embossed,
	debossed, engraved, foil blocked, die-cut,
	perforated, scored, and drilled
	spiral bound

"The Science of Sensation" was designed to visually illustrate every aspect of print production available from this Atlanta-based print company. Housed within a sturdy slipcase, the full Canadian-bound brochure sits with its spine protruding by 25mm (1in). Each of the 16 pages is French-folded, with the bottom edge sealed to form a pocket. These pockets contain cards which elaborate upon the one-line questions posed on the outside of the page.

Design	Sagmeister Inc.
Project	Zumtobel AG 01/02
Specification	112 pages plus cover
	printed 5-color process
	thread-sewn sections

The cover of this annual report for the lighting company Zumtobel features special plastic extrusions on both front and back covers. The front cover has a vase of flowers and the back, the title of the report. The "still life" image on the front is used within the book as a subject to showcase the various special lighting effects that the company is capable of producing. The uncovered spine holds the company's name, which is formed by printing fragments of type on each of the folded sections of the report; once bound together, these fragments align to form the words. Inside, the clean, typographic text pages are printed in black and a special pale blue/gray; these pages contrast with the strong, full-bleed photography that appears throughout the book.

3-D plastics

This annual report features special plastic extrusions on both front and back covers. The front cover has a vase of flowers and the back, the title of the report. The title also appears on the book's exposed spine, formed by printing fragments of the letters on the folded sections of the book.

Design	Underware/Piet Schreuders
Project	Sauna: Read Naked
Specification	48 pages plus cover
	printed 4-color process plus specials
	Singer-sewn through

This type-specimen book goes beyond the realms of the standard 4-page leaflet often sent out to announce a new font design. The name of the font, Sauna, is the starting point for this elaborate production. Printed on a special stock that is capable of withstanding temperatures of up to 120ºC (248ºF), some pages are printed with a special humidity-controlled ink that only becomes visible inside a sauna, where it reveals hidden messages. The covers are French-folded around a stiff sheet of card; this allows the same stock to be used throughout the book while giving the covers more stability.

The book is Singer-sewn through, a binding method that is incredibly strong and which, as it requires no glues, is able to withstand extreme temperature changes.

French-folded covers

The covers are French-folded around a stiff sheet of card; this allows the same stock to be used throughout the book while giving the covers more stability. The book is Singer-sewn through, a binding method that is incredibly strong and which, as it requires no glues, is able to withstand extreme temperature changes.

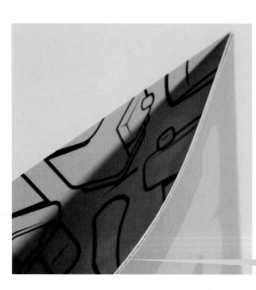

Design	Spin
Project	**Kunst Deutsche Bank: Visuell 25**
Specification	**308 pages plus 4-page cover**
	printed 4-color process plus 2 specials
	perfect-bound

Produced as a magazine, though with a page count in excess of 300, this publication takes on the proportions of a book or catalog. Published in English and German imprints, the book is a vehicle for the Deutsche Bank's extensive art interest. The predominantly 4-color process printing is complemented with metallic silver and fluorescent pink.

Design	A2-GRAPHICS/SW/HK
Project	ISTD TypoGraphic 60, "Primal Typography"
Specification	64 pages plus 8-page dust jacket and bookbinding boards
	printed 2 colors and 4-color process
	woodblock printed
	saddle-stitched

This edition of the journal looks like a casebound book, but in fact the journal has simply been saddle-stitched, and gray bookbinding boards have been bonded to the front and back covers to give the publication more stability and bulk. These boards have then been covered with a woodblock-printed dust jacket.

Woodblock type has been combined with conventional offset litho throughout the journal. The word "typography" has been printed through the book; starting with the first two letters on the front cover, the remaining letters are printed on the contents, the editorial pages, the endmatter, and the back cover.

Design	Design Project
Project	The Process of Printing
Specification	46 pages plus casebound cover with two-thirds slipcase printed 1 color and 4-color process plus 5 metallics, 5 fluorescents, and UV varnishes foil blocked, die-cut, embossed thread-sewn sections

Produced as a promotional book for a printing firm, this book showcases the vast array of specialist printing processes and finishes available from the company. The first 16-page section is printed on a pale green, uncoated stock in fluorescent green. It features a series of coarse, halftone reproductions of photographs taken in the printing works, together with information about the company and its methodology. This section is followed by a series of colored plates printed on a more substantial, coated silk stock. These provide graphic examples of the creative potential of overprinting process colors, of metallics, fluorescents, die-cutting, embossing, and foil blocking. The book is casebound in a white buckram cloth with the title foil blocked in a holographic silver. The white cover is complemented by a two-thirds dust jacket printed in a series of color bands.

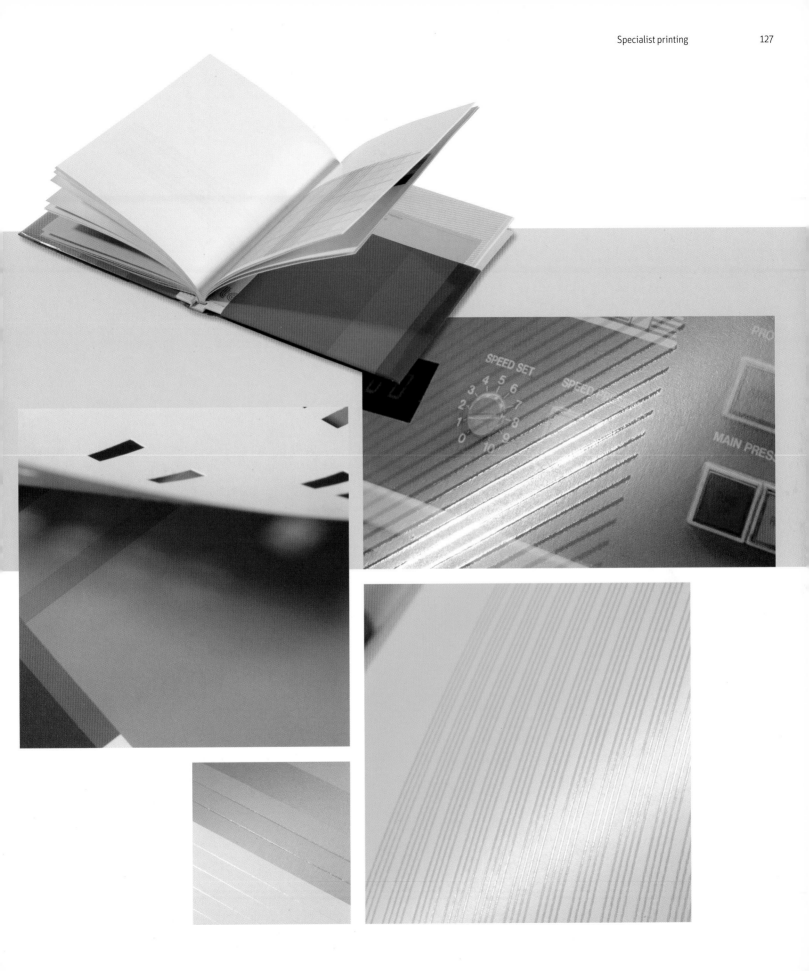

Design	Base Design
Project	En Casa II
Specification	printed 4-color process
	laser cut
	binding screws

For the second consecutive year, La Casa Encendida celebrated its anniversary with a book showcasing a selection of artists' work. The artists were asked to contribute work to the book with consideration to the book's format. Each artist used different stocks and printing processes, including laser die-cuts and varnishes. As the book is bound with three binding screws, a great level of flexibility was possible.

Folding and finishing

Design	sans+baum
Project	ISTD TypoGraphic 59, "Back to Type"
Specification	40 pages plus 4-page cover
	printed 4-color process plus 6 colors
	French-folded, perfect-bound

This edition of the everchanging type journal features a clever series of folded pages, printed in colors that are combined to get the maximum from special colors and 4-color reproductions.

The elaborate pagination of the journal works in such a way as to switch between perforated French-folds and standard single pages. The outside of each page is purely typographic, printed in a range of special colors. Once the perforated French-folds have been torn open, images for each of the essays are revealed. Most of the image sections are printed in 2 special colors, with 4-color spreads used where necessary.

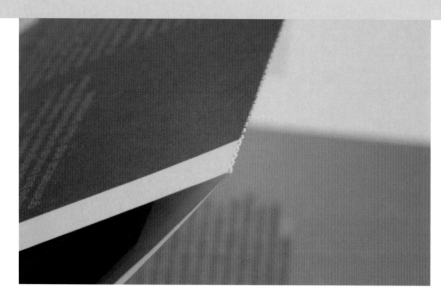

Perforated folds

The outside of each French-folded page is purely typographic, printed in a range of special colors. Once the perforated page has been torn open, images for each of the essays are revealed. Printed 2 spot colors or 4-color process, depending on subject matter.

Design	Kapitza
Project	**What does it mean when a whole culture dreams the same dream?**
Specification	**120 French-folded pages plus 8-page cover printed as 5 single-color sections French-folded, perfect-bound**

For an exhibition of three text-based artists, Kapitza took charge of the visual manifestation of their written words. The exhibition was formed by a series of 15 A1 (594 x 841mm/23⅜ x 33⅛in) posters, each with a text printed in a single color. The designer worked with just one dot-matrix font for the entire project. The selected font is simply constructed from a square base element, which has the advantage of allowing the typeface to be scaled up and down and to maintain a relationship with other letters at different sizes. The catalog accompanying the exhibition was simply formed by cutting, folding, and binding the 15 posters, thereby making catalog and exhibition one

entity. Five different Pantone colors were used for the posters, which helps add pace and variation to the bound catalog edition. The designer has created the posters in such a way that when they appear in the bound edition they are still intact and readable. This is achieved by making the text appear at different scales on the same sheets, allowing for legibility at different distances.

Design	Mode
Project	Dalton Maag: Font Book Collection 01
Specification	200 pages plus 4-page cover and dust jacket
	printed 2 colors
	perforated
	saddle-stitched

This font catalog focuses on four type families designed by Dalton Maag. Each font is shown in a variety of weights and combinations of size, for text and headline setting. All pages are printed in the two corporate colors of pale, duck-egg blue and dark blue on a very light bible paper. Because this weight of paper allows for a great deal of showthrough, only the recto pages are printed. The designers have made full use of the translucent paper by printing solid areas of color on some pages to hide and reveal elements of the following pages. All the text pages have a series of vertical, perforated lines running down them, the positions of which are in line with the typographic grid. These perforations allow the user either to fold back pages to show different combinations of weight and size, or to tear out perforated strips for use as sample swatches.

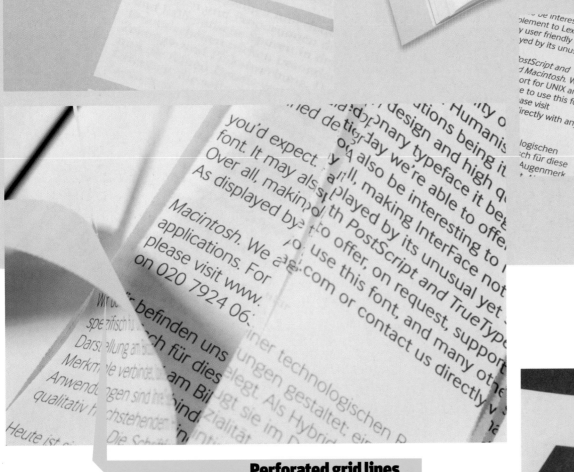

Perforated grid lines

The catalog features a series of vertical perforated lines running down the page, the positions of which are in line with the typographic grid. These perforations allow the user either to fold back pages, or to tear out perforated strips for use as sample swatches.

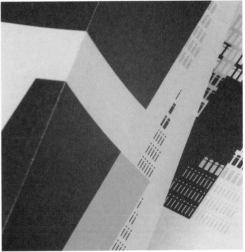

Design	Irma Boom
Project	Grafisch Nederland 2005 Kleur
Specification	168 pages
	printed 4-color process plus 80 special Pantone colors
	perforated
	perfect-bound

Based on the theme of "color," Irma Boom was given total freedom to develop this book for the KVGO (the Dutch Association of the Graphic Industry). She selected 80 works of art by various artists ranging from Jan Vermeer to Andy Warhol. Each image was fragmented into a series of color bars that depict the original painting's palette. These abstracted paintings are concealed within the perforated sections of the book. The pages must be torn open in order to reveal the "image." On the outside of these folded sections are a series of flat color fields printed in a vast array of Pantone inks.

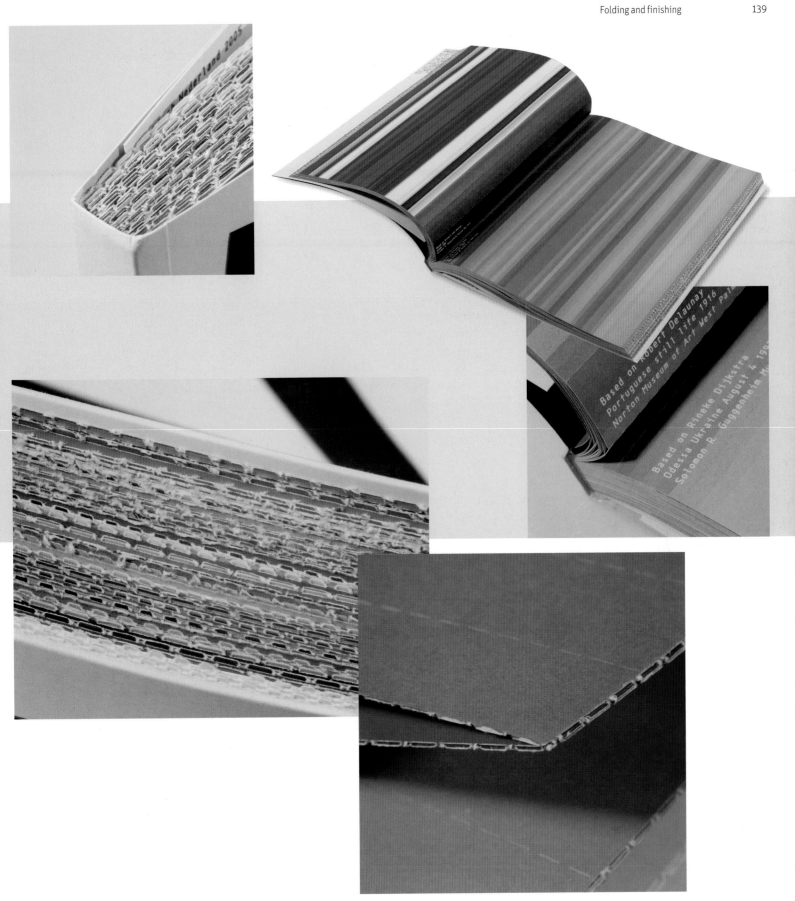

Design	Karel Martens
Project	Counterprint
Specification	**64-page text section plus 16-page folded cover** **printed 4-color process** **perfect-bound**

Featuring the beautiful, self-initiated printed works of the Dutch graphic designer and teacher Karel Martens, this book has an unfinished quality to it—the sheets, which are printed only on one face, have been folded and bound into the book without the top folded edge being trimmed off. As a result, the book feels like a collection of seemingly random elements, with great contrasts of scale and color.

The cover is produced as a large printed sheet, printed 4-color process on one side, with the other printed in black only. The color work is folded inside the cover, requiring a degree of care to unfold it to see the full scale of the sheet without tearing the cover away from the main body of the book.

Untrimmed edges

The sections, which are printed only on one face, have been folded and bound into the book without the top folded edge being trimmed.

Design	MadeThought
Project	The Piano Factory
Specification	30 pages plus 8-page cover
	printed 4-color process
	concertina-folded sections

Produced to promote an office development in central London, this understated brochure plays with black-on-black printing, both on the cover and inside. The cover is simply printed in black, with a match varnish used to create a silhouette of trees and foliage, giving it a nocturnal quality. Inside, the text pages are revealed as a long concertina-folded section, with all the text reversed out in white. Full-color photographs are used throughout the catalog, with sections of the images overprinted with black, which again gives a dark, nocturnal quality to the brochure. The flipside of this concertina is also printed in solid black.

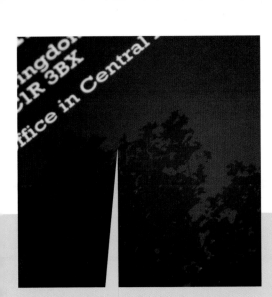

Black overprint

Throughout the brochure, images are overprinted in solid black. This gives the impression of a subtle varnish, and renders the images barely visible.

Design	MadeThought
Project	Reiss: Womenswear Lookbook Autumn/Winter 2005/06
Specification	**2 folded 8-page sections plus bellyband cover**
	printed 4-color process
	concertina-folded

Working simply with catwalk shots of both womenswear
and menswear, this fashion "lookbook" is printed on a
high-gloss board. The two concertina-folded sections are
held together by a black bellyband, with the text screenprinted white onto the matte black rubberized material.

Design	Struktur Design
Project	Bluebridge
Specifications	18 pages, self cover
	printed 2 colors
	folded

This simple brochure for a London-based human resources company uses its identity as a basis for its format, with the lime-green square of the logo repeated on the cover. The brochure is formed from a series of staggered concertina folds, with a strip of each spread visible from the front cover. As each folded section is opened, information is revealed about the company, but the large green square remains complete.

Design	Nokia Design Brand Team
Project	Nokia Annual Report
Specification	12 pages plus 20 small inset pages and 4-page cover
	printed 5 colors and 6 colors
	French-folded, perfect-bound

This annual report for the mobile phone company Nokia combines two different formats that carry different levels of information. The large French-folded pages feature a series of informal photographs of a variety of people printed onto a light weight of coated silk stock. No type is printed on these pages (with the exception of page numbers), although a series of large typographic statements are printed in mirror image on the inside of the French-folded pages, and are just legible through the light paper. A series of smaller pages are bound into the bottom of the brochure, printed on an uncoated stock, and feature the more conventional annual report information.

French-folded

A series of large typographic
statements are printed in mirror
image on the inside of the French-
folded pages, and are just legible
through the light paper.

Design	Spin
Project	**Mark Alexander: The Bigger Victory**
Specification	**54 pages plus casebound cover**
	printed 4-color process
	thread-sewn sections

This elegantly understated artist's catalog for an
exhibition at the Haunch of Venison gallery in London
is fairly conventional throughout, with the exception
of a large, foldout section which shows a series of five
paintings. In this the left page has a conventional, single-
page foldout, while the right page has two additional pages
that fold back on themselves. The way the pages are folded
allows the unopened spread to appear with an image on
the right page, as they do through the rest of the catalog.
The cover features a quality gray cloth with the artist's
name and the exhibition title foil blocked in white and
yellow on both cover and spine. Yellow is also used for
the head- and tailbands on the binding.

Design	Spin
Project	**Changes of Mind: Belief and Transformation**
Specification	**16 pages plus cover**
	printed 4-color process
	saddle-stitched

Each of the eight artists in this group show at the Haunch of Venison gallery in London is given their own font. These fonts appear on the cover as a typographic list and also on the artist's respective spreads inside the catalog. The cover is simply printed in black, with a series of interlocking grid lines printed on the front and back. The grid is based on the image boxes used for every artist inside the catalog. The left edge of the cover features a 75mm (3in) flap. This flap system appears on all the right-hand pages, and is used to contain the artist's name along with the credits for the illustrated works.

Design	Christine Fent/Manja Hellpap/Gilmar Wendt
Project	ISTD: International Typographic Awards 2004
Specification	108 pages plus 4-page cover and dust jacket printed 4-color process plus metallic gold thread-sewn sections

The results of the 2004 awards from the International Society of Typographic Designers were published in this understated small book. It contains all the usual images of the judging process—chin rubbing, head scratching, and lively interactions—shot in black-and-white. The award winners' work is all shown in full color, shot in a casual manner, with credits printed in black and gold. The end leaves of the book use a thin, black, uncoated stock with the text printed in gold. Gold is also used on the cropped dust jacket, with a gold vignette bleeding up the page. The title is also printed on the cream-colored cover board.

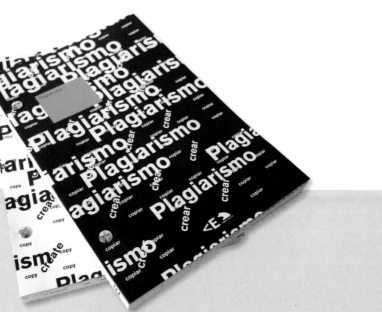

Design	Base Design
Project	Plagiarismo
Specification	16 pages plus cover
	printed 4-color process
	saddle-stitched

This catalog was produced to accompany an exhibition about plagiarism in a variety of different creative fields (including art, music, film, architecture, and design) held at La Casa Encendida in Spain. The catalog was designed for three versions: two printed editions, one in English and one in Castilian, with a third version developed as a series of A3 (420 x 297mm/16^1/$_2$ x 11^3/$_4$in), black-and-white, photocopiable sheets. This edition was free and formed part of the exhibition, at which there was a photocopying machine and the necessary elements for binding the loose sheets. The A3 sheets were designed to be folded twice down to an A5 (210 x 148mm/8^1/$_4$ x 5^7/$_8$in) format, then bound together to form the catalog.

Binding

Design	SEA Design
Project	Wim Crouwel: Seen Unseen
Specification	32 pages plus 4-page cover
	printed 4-color process plus metallics and fluorescents
	sewn sections with bookbinders' cloth

This was produced to accompany an exhibition of classic posters by the Dutch high priest of design, Wim Crouwel. The cover plays with a font designed by Crouwel for the artist Claes Oldenburg in 1970; the thin outline version of the font printed in orange on the cover is beautifully embossed. This process adds greatly to the cover, giving a far more tactile quality to the catalog. The inside front cover, which is printed in a vignetted metallic copper, allows the fine embossing work to shine and adds to the overall look of the project. Inside, eight posters from Crouwel's archives are illustrated, together with comments from contemporary designers, printed in 4-color process with the text printed in metallic copper. The back section of the catalog shows Crouwel's Soft Alphabet in full, printed in fluorescent orange and metallic copper.

The catalog is bound in thread-sewn sections, with a white bookbinders' cloth tape applied to the cover of the spine. This text block is then glued to the inside back cover, enabling the front cover to open flat to reveal the binding tape.

Binding tape

A white, cloth bookbinders' tape
is applied to the cover of the
spine. The text block is then glued
to the inside back cover, enabling
the front cover to open flat to
reveal the binding tape.

Design	**Spin**
Project	**Animals**
Specification	**72 pages plus casebound cover**
	printed 4-color process with 2-color sections
	sewn sections

Produced to accompany a group art exhibition at the London gallery, Haunch of Venison, the essays and plate sections of this catalog have been segregated by the designers into two different formats within the casebound covers. The essays are printed onto a gray uncoated stock at a reduced format, and this small 16-page section is bound into the main body of the book just after the endpapers at the front of the catalog. The neutral gray color of the stock contrasts with the bright magenta ink used for the first of the two essays, and this in turn is complemented by the black ink used for the second essay. This reduced-size section is followed by the main plate section of the catalog, which is printed in full color onto a coated gloss stock. At the back of the catalog is a 20-page section, again using uncoated gray stock, but this time produced at a full-page format. This back section features a short biography for each of the 17 selected artists, the text being positioned within the same reduced-size area that was used for the essay section at the front of the book, with the remainder of the page occupied by a series of gridded black dots that represent the positions of the images in the plate section.

Design	B+B
Project	Artomatic: Library
Specification	**10 pages**
	screenprinted in 4 colors
	tipped-in label and holographic sticker
	plastic comb binding

Printed on 2mm-thick bookbinding gray board, this book—produced to promote a print/research library resource—has a childlike quality to it. By virtue of the screenprinting process, the book's drab gray board is enlivened through the use of bright red, pale blues, soft yellows, and white. The book has a tipped-in label on the inside front cover, referencing traditional library tickets. It is bound using a clear plastic comb, a binding system that is seen less and less frequently today.

Design	Secondary Modern
Project	Jeff Luke: Use
Specification	48 pages plus 6 tabbed index dividers and 4-page cover
	printed 1 color and 4-color process
	half Canadian bound

Featuring the work of the late Jeff Luke, this catalog has been sympathetically designed to reflect the style and ideas of the artist. It features six thumb-tabbed dividers printed in black on an uncoated buff card, and this— combined with the half Canadian binding—gives the catalog the appearance of a user's manual. The sections are printed on various stocks (uncoated; coated silk; and fibrous, uncoated gray), in black and 4-color process.

Half Canadian binding

The catalog is half Canadian bound, a process where the text pages are wire-bound into the back of the cover, this allows the spine and front cover to remain clean with no visible sign of the wire.

Design	Base Design
Project	Amat Finques
Specification	16 pages plus 8-page cover
	printed 4-color process and 6 colors
	Singer-sewn section

Printed in Spanish, Portuguese, and English, this simple brochure for a Spanish estate agent works with three key colors to separate the languages: red, warm gray, and a tint of black. The brochure is printed on a soft, off-white, uncoated stock that prevents the clean typographic cover treatment from becoming too cold and hard. As a contrast to the understated cover, the inside front and back flaps are printed full bleed in a vibrant warm yellow. Inside, the colored typographic treatment is illustrated with a series of full-page images of selected key properties from the company's portfolio. The quality of the brochure is further enhanced by the binding technique, with red, Singer-sewn thread used as a more elegant alternative to the more conventional saddle-stitched option.

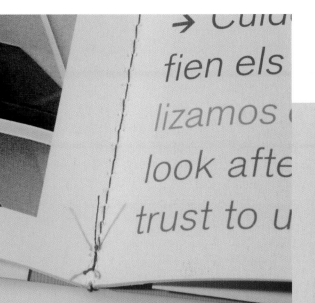

Design	Emmi
Project	Emmi's Portfolio
Specification	58 pages plus 4-page cover
	printed 4-color process
	thread-sewn sections (hand-finished)

Created as a self-promotional piece for the designers,
this brochure groups together a variety of samples of work,
with each project shown at a different size and format
from the next. Each project also has a sheet of preprinted
ruled paper that is used as a divider wrap, and is produced
at a different physical size. Each of the sections is thread-
sewn into the card cover, using different-colored thread
for each project.

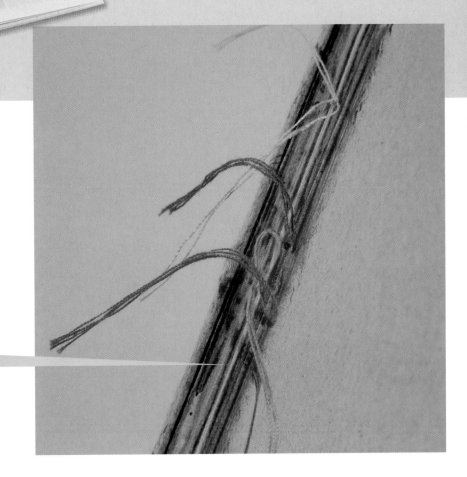

Hand sewn

Each of the sections is thread sewn by hand into the card cover, using different-colored thread for each project. As the thread is sewn through the grayboard cover, the spine becomes decorated with the multicolored threads.

Design	BB/Saunders
Project	Centrefold 2
Specification	56 pages
	printed 4-color process
	unbound

Sealed within a black envelope, with the edges sewn together, this fashion biannual has an air of exclusivity and mystery. With no obvious sign of entry, the reader is left to cut or tear the beautiful packaging open to find out more. The envelope is printed with two blacks: the first is printed full bleed with the text white out, the second is used for fine-line illustration work. On the inside of the envelope is an image printed in black and silver, which is only fully visible if all three sewn sides of the envelope are opened. The magazine itself consists of a series of folded sheets that are left unbound, allowing the reader to view the pages as a conventional magazine or to remove and view them as individual sheets. Large page numbers are printed in the top corner of each page, grouped together to state the page numbers of each sheet, for example, 2/55 appears on page two, as this also refers to page 55, which is on the same sheet of paper. The magazine is printed on a high-quality, very smooth, uncoated stock with the central four pages printed on a gloss stock.

Loose-leaf

The magazine consists of a series of folded sheets that are left unbound, allowing the reader to view the pages as a conventional magazine or to remove and view them as individual sheets.

Design	Purtill Family Business
Project	Richard Tuttle: In Parts: 1998–2001
Specification	**52 pages plus 4-page cover** **printed 2 colors and 4-color process** **4-page sections folded down and bound**

Produced to accompany an exhibition of Richard Tuttle's work at the Institute of Contemporary Art, University of Pennsylvania, this catalog is formed from 13 sheets of paper, each of which is folded twice to give an 8-page section. These sections are bound down the folded edge using a strong, flexible, rubberized glue, to form the book onto which the front and back covers are drawn. As is illustrated on the cover, the 13 sections each represent a seasonal period of the artist's work from 1998 to 2001. This method of binding allows the pages to unfold to a larger format, which reveals large details of the artist's work. Each folded section has a fragment of type printed in black on the folded edge; with all the sections bound, these fragments join together to form the artist's name.

Foldout sections

The book is formed by a series of sheets, each of which is folded twice to form 8-page sections. These sections are bound together using a flexible adhesive. The pages work both as a conventional book and also as foldout sections. The spine typography is constructed from fragments printed on each of the folded sections.

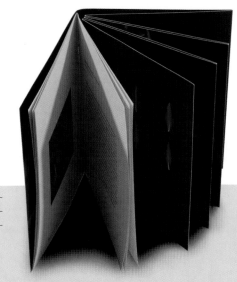

Design	Rose Design
Project	Barbara and Zafer Baran: The Flower Cabinet
Specification	16 pages plus 12-page folded section
	printed mono and 4-color process
	saddle-stitched and folded

This elegant little booklet, produced for an exhibition of the husband-and-wife photo artists at the Blue Gallery in London, combines essays and images in an unusual manner. The 16-page essay section is printed onto a gray uncoated stock, as a saddle-stitched section that is stapled into the folded card cover. The essays are printed in dark gray only on a delicate lightweight paper. The images are printed in full color with a machine varnish on top, onto a heavy card stock that forms the cover, with a 12-panel concertina section at the back.

Concertina folded

This small booklet combines both a saddle-stitched section and a concertina-folded section. The 16-page, saddle-stitched section is tipped-in to the cover, which extends into a 12-panel, concertina-folded element.

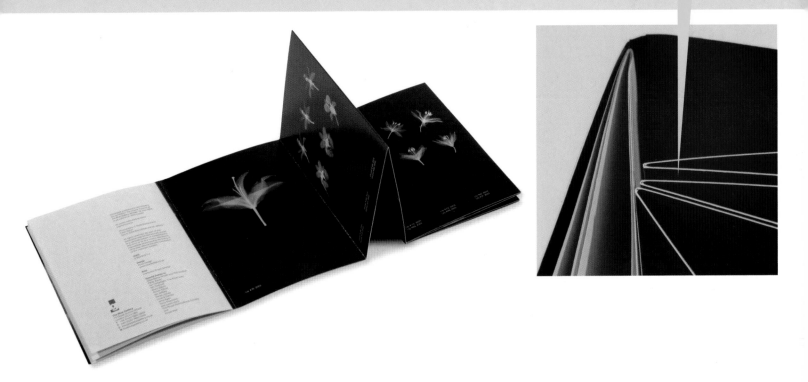

Design	Eg.G
Project	Quarantine portfolio brochure
Specification	**20 pages plus 6-page cover**
	printed black and 4-color process
	binding screws

Produced for a theater production company, this small booklet features the group's projects, ideas, and research. The text section uses a strong yellow to highlight various extracts from the text, either with white blocks behind the black text on a full-bleed yellow background, or yellow blocks behind the black text on a white background. Small, 4-color reproductions appear throughout the booklet, showing elements from the various productions. The 6-page cover wraps around from the inside back, where it is bound to the main body of the book with binding screws. The outside of the cover is simply printed in black, with the inside printed full-bleed yellow.

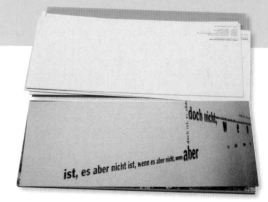

Design	Projekttriangle
Project	Form+Farbe
Specification	26 pages plus cover boards
	printed 1 color
	rubber stamped
	loose-leaf

The binding of this artist's brochure has been stripped back to the simplest method possible. The series of loose pages are sandwiched between two sheets of thick, gray board and held together with a thick, red rubber band. Color is kept to a minimum; with the exception of one red page, everything else is printed in black only. A sheet of thick yellow tracing paper is included to add color to the book. The reader is encouraged to play with the order and sequence of the pages, allowing a great deal of freedom. The front cover simply has the title rubber stamped in brown—a cheap, yet striking method that extends the feeling of the book's limited-edition quality.

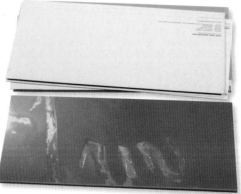

Design	Base Design
Project	Women'secret: Look Book Spring/Summer 2003
Specification	24 pages plus 4-page cover/
	16 pages plus 4-page cover
	printed 4-color process
	French-folded, held with elastic band

This fashion book is broken into two separate booklets, both with the same format. The French-folded pages are bound together simply with an elastic band held in place by notches cut into the top and bottom of the pages and cover. This binding method allows the pages a good degree of flexibility and movement as they are turned, and also allows for the option of removing and reassembling the pages. The books are printed 4-color throughout with the left page of each spread blank, allowing the images to appear in isolation.

Design	Spin
Project	Jorge Pardo
Specification	**3 sections of 16 pages plus 4-page cover**
	printed 1 color and 5 colors
	clear PVC wallet
	thread-sewn sections

This catalog, produced to accompany an exhibition of the sculptor's work at the Haunch of Venison gallery in Zurich, Switzerland, is formed by three 16-page sections, each with its own cover. These three sections are thread-sewn together to form a whole. The delicacy of the sewing remains visible on the spine, however, the catalog is protected by a clear, PVC wallet. The first section is printed on a creamy, off-white, uncoated stock in 4-color process plus an earthy red, which is used for the text. This section includes a series of photographs showing the construction process of the sculpture—a life-size yacht. The second section is printed on a clean white version of the same stock, printed in the same five colors. This section shows a selection of images from previous installations. The final section, which is text only, reverts to the off-white stock and is printed just in red ink. Each of the three sections has its own cover, all printed in red onto an orange, uncoated stock.

Thread sewing

The three thread-sewn booklets are carefully bound together with additional thread to form a delicate book. This method allows the three booklets to open freely and maintain their own individuality. The book is protected by a clear PVC dust jacket.

Design	Thorsten Romanus
Project	Jean Prouvé | Charles & Ray Eames: Constructive Furniture
Specification	80 pages plus 4-page cover and 8-page dust jacket printed 4-color process plus 1 special thread-sewn sections

Produced by the Swiss-based, classic furniture company Vitra, this book showcases the work of French designer Jean Prouvé and American husband-and-wife team Charles and Ray Eames. It is printed 4-color process plus warm gray onto an uncoated stock. A series of strong, flat colors, derived from the designers' work, are printed full bleed as section dividers. The cover is printed in a solid green, both inside and out, with a beautiful 8-page dust jacket. The dust jacket is formed from high-quality red cloth bonded to a green card. The result is a book that has the tactile qualities of a casebound volume with the flexibility of a paperback.

Cloth dust jacket

The dust jacket is formed from a high-quality red cloth which is bonded to a green card. This gives the book the tactile qualities of a casebound volume with the flexibility of a paperback.

Design	Spin
Project	Kienholz
Specification	96 pages
	printed 4-color process plus one special
	thread-sewn sections

Produced to accompany an exhibition of the husband-and-wife artists held at the Haunch of Venison in London, this art catalog is fairly conventional in format, except that the cover boards have been trimmed flush to the text pages, which gives the book a solid, hard edge. The grayboards have a cool gray paper bonded to them; this wraps around the spine which adds to the clean lines of the cover. Warm gray is printed full bleed inside to divide sections, and is also used in the text pages.

Trimmed flush

The gray cover boards have a cool gray paper bonded to them which wraps around the spine. The boards have been trimmed flush to the text pages, giving the book a solid, hard edge.

Design	Base Design
Project	Jorge Macchi: Doppelgangers
Specification	96 pages
	printed 4-color process plus one special
	Singer-sewn through

This catalog was produced to accompany an exhibition of the work of Argentinian artist Jorge Macchi at La Casa Encendida in Spain. The exhibition was called Doppelgangers, and the catalog follows the same theme. The artist chose a story by Edgar Allan Poe, "William Wilson," and this story runs throughout the catalog in a fairly conventional manner. However, on closer inspection it is found that the French-folded pages can be unfolded to reveal a series of images by the artist. These images are mirrored on a central axis, echoing the idea of the Doppelganger. The catalog is Singer-sewn through and has a cover with a conventional spine applied.

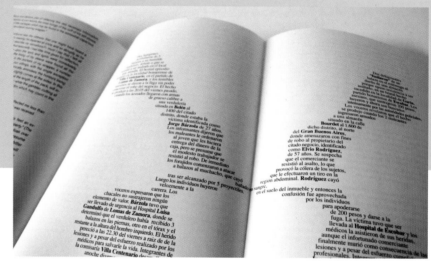

Design	MadeThought
Project	Established & Sons: 2005 Collection
Specification	20 pages of text with 16-page insert plus 4-page cover printed 4-color process plus 1 color saddle-stitched

This catalog for British product design company Established & Sons features a star-studded list of product designers and architects in its stable. The cover is printed on a cast-coated stock, with the matte, uncoated surface on the outside and the shiny surface forming the inside front and back. It is printed in a single red color, which is picked up on the text pages of the catalog as a fifth color. Inside, the images of the various products and furniture are left clear, with no text details printed on them, except for a running head at the top of the page. All product information appears on a thin, uncoated, reduced-size page, which is printed in the same red as is used elsewhere; a tint of the red is also printed over the entire surface of this smaller page, giving the impression of a pink-colored stock.

Inset pages

Information for all products is printed onto a reduced-format page, which is bound into the saddle-stitched brochure. These pages are printed onto a light weight of uncoated stock, trimmed flush to the bottom of the book.

Glossary

Bible paper

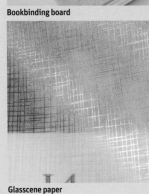

Bookbinding board

Glasscene paper

Polypropylene

MATERIALS

Bible paper
A very thin paper, usually 40–60gsm, used for (among other things) bibles, directories, and dictionaries.

Bookbinding board
A dense fiberboard used for the covers of casebound books.

Cast-coated
Paper that has a very high-quality, high-gloss surface on one side, while the reverse remains matte and uncoated.

Coated stock
A smooth, hard-surfaced paper good for reproducing halftone images. It is created by coating the surface with china clay.

Glasscene paper
A thin, semi-transparent paper often used in photograph albums to protect the images.

Polypropylene
A flexible plastic sheet available in many different colors, including clear and frosted.

Simulator paper
A thin, translucent paper, more commonly known as tracing paper.

Stock
The paper or other material on which a book is printed.

Uncoated stock
Paper that has a rougher surface than coated paper, and which is both bulkier and more opaque.

PRINTING

Bit-map
A generic style of computer-originated typefaces, constructed pixel by pixel. The term is also used to describe the pixilation of a digital image.

Bleed
The term used to refer to an element printed beyond the trimmed edge of the page, allowing the image, rule, or type to extend to the very edge of the printed page.

CMYK
See: Inks

Duotone
Where two colors are printed together to make an image richer and denser in color.

Four-color process
(4-color process)
See: Inks.

Halftone
A process used to reproduce an illustration, which involves breaking it up into small dots of different densities to simulate a full tonal range.

Simulator paper

Uncoated stock

Bit-map

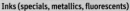

Inks (specials, metallics, fluorescents)

Inks (specials, metallics, fluorescents)
Almost all mass-produced books are printed using lithographic inks. As a rule, full-color printing is achieved through the combination of four process colors: cyan, magenta, yellow, and black/key (CMYK). However, additional "special" inks—such as fluorescents or metallics to create shiny, gold, or silver effects—can also be used to produce distinctive results.

Letterpress

Letterpress
A traditional method of printing type, using a series of metal stamps with individual letters cast into the surface. The letters are set into a form, inked up, and pressed onto the paper's surface. The printed sheet becomes more tactile than that produced by conventional offset lithographic printing, because the type becomes debossed into the surface.

Raster imaging

Process colors
See: Inks.

Raster imaging
An alternative method of halftone screening using an electron beam. It creates complex, irregular patterns of very fine dots and produces higher-quality images and color work.

Reversed type

Reversed type
The letters are left unprinted, and the surrounding area is printed. This allows the type to reveal the base color of the stock.

Screenprinting

RGB
Red, Green, Blue. The three primary colors used on screen to generate a full spectrum of color.

Screenprinting
A printing method that applies ink onto the surface of the material with a squeegee through a fine silk mesh. This achieves a much denser application of ink than lithography and may be used on an almost limitless variety of surfaces.

Spot color
A special color not generated by the 4-color process method.

Vignette
Or graduated tint. Where one color fades into another color or white.

Woodblock type
Letters carved in pieces of wood to be relief-printed—similar to letterpress. Traditionally woodblock type was used for headline and poster work.

FOLDING

Concertina folded
Pages folded in a zigzag manner, like the bellows of a concertina.

French-fold
The method of folding a page in half and binding along the open edges.

Vignette

Woodblock type

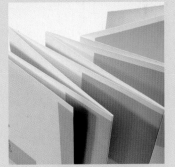

Concertina folded

French-fold

188

Perforated folds

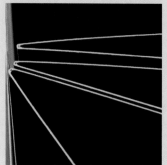
Roll folding

Debossed

Die-cut

Perforated folds
Printed sheets are perforated prior to folding the sheets down to the final page size. This allows the French-fold pages to be torn open easily.

Roll folding
A process whereby a long sheet of paper is folded into panels or pages starting from the far right, with each subsequent panel folded back toward the left—effectively it is rolled back around itself.

FINISHING

Debossed
Having a surface pattern pressed into the page. This process is also known as blind embossing.

Die-cut
The method by which intricate shapes can be cut from the page. This process requires a custom-made die, which has a sharp steel edge constructed to cut the required shape.

Embossed
Having a raised surface pattern. This is created by using a male and female form.

Foil blocking
A printing method that transfers a metallic foil to the page through the application of a metal block and heat.

Lamination
The application of a clear matte or gloss protective film over the printed surface of a sheet of paper.

Laser die-cut
A very precise method of cutting out elements from stock, highly creative shapes can be successfully cut in the page, way beyond the abilities of conventional die-cutting.

Pigment blocking
A process similar to foil blocking, but using colored film.

Thermography
A relief effect created by dusting a special powder onto a printed image while still wet, then passing the sheet through a heating device.

Embossed

Foil blocking

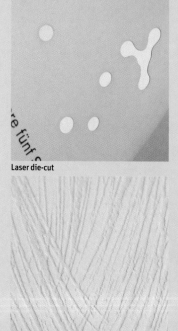
Laser die-cut

Thermography

UV varnish

UV varnish

A plastic-based varnish applied by screenprinting, and available in matte, satin, and gloss finishes. It can be applied over the entire surface or treated as a spot varnish, enabling the designer to print elements purely as a varnish or to highlight selected elements on the page.

BINDING

Bellyband

A strip of paper or other material that wraps around the center of the book to prevent the pages from opening.

Binding screws

Small brass thumb screws consisting of a male and female part, and used to bind loose sheets together. They are generally available in brass or nickel-plated (silver).

Burstbound section

A method of binding similar to a thread-sewn section, whereby the sections of a book are gathered, but instead of being sewn with thread, the folded edges are perforated and then glue is permitted to penetrate the fold. This method is stronger than

perfect binding, but not as strong as a thread-sewn section. The pages can be opened moderately flat, but if excess pressure is applied, the binding may crack.

Casebound

The term used for a hardback book.

Comb binding

Similar in principle to wire binding, a machine is used to punch a row of small holes along the edge of the book, a plastic "comb" is then pushed through the holes to create the binding.

Flush-trimmed cover

Where a casebound book has its cover boards trimmed flush to the text pages, creating a smooth, crisp finish.

Half Canadian binding

A method similar to wire binding, although the cover has a spine and the wire is bound through the back cover, which has two additional crease folds.

Bellyband

Binding screws

Burstbound section

Casebound

Comb binding

Flush-trimmed cover

Half Canadian binding

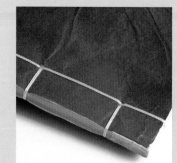

Japanese binding

Loose-leaf

Perfect binding

Saddle-stitching

Japanese binding
A binding method whereby the thread is bound from the back to the front of the book and around the outside edge of the spine. It is ideal for binding loose sheets.

Loose-leaf
A collection of unbound pages.

Perfect binding
A binding method in which pages in the gatherings of a book are notched along their uncut edges, to be glued together into the spine. The result is not usually as strong as a thread-sewn volume. However, this method allows for greater flexibility in the number of pages, and enables a variety of different stocks and printed sheets to be compiled in different sequences.

Saddle-stitching
The standard method for binding brochures and magazines. The process involves gathering the pages to be bound and stapling them through the folded edges.

Sewn through
A method of binding by sewing through the front of a book to the back on an industrial version of the household sewing machine. It is used mainly on loose-leaf and French-folded documents.

Singer-sewn
A method of binding by sewing along the centerfold of a document on an industrial version of the household sewing machine. Used as an attractive alternative to saddle-stitching.

Thread-sewn section
A method of binding by sewing the different gathered sections of a book together with thread. This gives a strong, durable binding, and enables the pages to be opened flat without any danger of damaging the binding. Also known as "sewn section."

Tipped-in
The term used to describe gluing supplementary paper into a book. It is often used to incorporate full-color plates into a mono-printed publication.

Sewn through

Singer-sewn

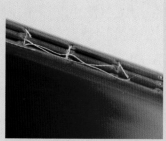

Thread-sewn stitch

Tipped-in

Wire binding

Wire binding

A binding method by which a thin spiral of wire is passed through a series of prepunched holes along the edge of the pages to be bound.

PARTS OF A BOOK

Dust jacket

A loose paper cover that protects the boards of a casebound book.

Endpapers

The first and last pages of a book, bonded to the inside of the hardback covers.

Fore-edge

The front or open edge of a book.

Head- and tailbands

A decorative strip of ribbon sewn into the back of the book block on a casebound book.

Imposition

The order in which pages are arranged so that, after printing and folding, the pages read in the correct sequence.

PLC cover

Printed Laminated Cover; a term used for casebound books that have a printed paper cover bonded onto the cover boards. Also known as PPC (Printed Paper Cover).

Prelims

The standard pages at the start of a book, including title page, publisher's credits, and contents page.

Recto

The front side of a sheet of paper, hence also a right-hand (odd-numbered) page of a book.

Self-cover

A term used to describe a brochure which uses the same stock for the cover as the text pages.

Slipcase

A protective box with one edge open, in which a book can be stored.

Verso

The reverse side of a sheet of paper, hence also a left-hand (even-numbered) page of a book.

Imposition

PLC cover

Self-cover

Dust jacket

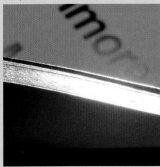

Fore-edge

Head- and tailbands

Slipcase

INDEX